GANDHI'S WAY

Gandhi's Way

A Handbook of Conflict Resolution

Updated with a New Preface and New Case Study

MARK JUERGENSMEYER

UNIVERSITY OF CALIFORNIA PRESS
Berkeley   Los Angeles   London

University of California Press
Berkeley and Los Angeles, California

University of California Press, Ltd.
London, England

This paperback is a substantially revised version of a work originally
published as *Fighting Fair with Gandhi* (San Francisco: Harper and Row,
1984) and then as *Fighting Fair* (San Francisco: Harper and Row, 1986).

Library of Congress Cataloging-in-Publication Data

Juergensmeyer, Mark.
   Gandhi's way : a handbook of conflict resolution,
updated with a new preface and new case study /
Mark Juergensmeyer. — [2005 ed.].
     p. cm.
   Previous ed.: 2002.
   Includes bibliographical references and index.
   ISBN 978-0-520-24497-9 (pbk. : alk. paper)
    1. Gandhi, Mahatma, 1869–1948—Political and
social views. 2. Conflict management. 3. Passive
resistance. 4. Nonviolence. I. Title.

DS481.G3J844 2005
303.6'1'0954—dc22   2004059886

Printed in the United States of America

15   14   13   12   11   10   09   08   07

10 9 8 7 6 5 4 3 2

The paper used in this publication is both acid-free and
totally chlorine-free (TCF). It meets the minimum requirements
of ANSI/NISO Z39.48-1992 (R 1997) (*Permanence of Paper*). ∞

to those with whom I have fought

Contents

Diagrams

Preface to the Revised Edition

Gandhi was a fighter. Whatever else one might say about him—that he was a saint, a clever politician, or a "seditious fakir," as Winston Churchill once put it—Gandhi certainly knew how to fight. In fact his approach to conflict and its resolution is one of Mohandas Gandhi's most enduring legacies.

For a pacifist, Gandhi was not very passive. "Where there is only a choice between cowardice and violence, I would advise violence," he once said, not because he welcomed bloodshed, but because he favored engagement.[1] He had little respect for passivity and even less for moral weakness.

To Gandhi, fighting had its benefits. An appreciation of other points of view enhances our own perspective. We are all limited by our own angle of vision, Gandhi said. Through fighting, one gains a broader view of truth.

This book is about Gandhi's way of dealing with conflict. It explores the basic principles of *satyagraha,* his method that encourages fighters to imagine solutions that include the best features of both sides and then fight in a way that is consistent with these goals, incorporating the solution into the struggle itself. He pioneered what is now called the "win-win" approach to conflict resolution.

The first third of this book is a primer. It is an attempt to give a straightforward introduction to Gandhi's way of fighting and a step-by-step set of rules to implement it. The second section of the book applies this method to a variety of real cases, from family disputes to political clashes involving terrorism. In the third section, Gandhi's ideas are challenged from Marxist, Freudian, and political realist positions, in a series of hypothetical conversations. Then the ideal Gandhi is pitted against the real one in a Gandhian critique of Gandhi himself.

I believe that Gandhi would have welcomed all of these encounters, even those offering the harshest criticisms of himself and his methods. For if one follows Gandhi's own advice, nothing should go unchallenged—not even what Gandhi himself did and thought. In fact, fighting with Gandhi is a fair and appropriate response to his way of thinking. It is in this spirit of intellectual *satyagraha* that I challenge Gandhi in the final section of this book.

The central tenets of Gandhi's way of conflict are straightforward: one should try to solve differences on the level of principles and one should adopt methods that are consistent with one's goals. As this book shows, these tenets can be applied to any kind of conflict, including everyday squabbles, tensions between family and friends, rivalries among social groups, and even ideological schisms that tear apart national and global societies.

Perhaps nothing tests an approach to resolving conflicts more severely than this latter kind of fighting. These conflicts can seem so basic, so intractable, and so vicious that no accommodation is possible. In the modern world, almost every generation has had to deal with such basic encounters between contesting world views.

During Gandhi's time, the struggle was against colonialism. Then came the Second World War, a contest between nationalism and imperialism. Later in the twentieth century, the Cold War between communism and capitalism was similarly regarded as an opposition impossible to resolve. In the early part of the twenty-first century this extreme antinomy has been characterized by the encounter between secular and religious politics. This new conflict has been dramatically punctuated by acts of terrorism on the one hand and militant efforts to wage a war against terrorism on the other.

As extreme as these conflicts are, they are still appropriate subjects for Gandhian analysis. In fact, Gandhi's principles of *satyagraha* were forged in the midst of an anti-colonial struggle. He also contended with the tensions of World War II, and once wrote an open letter to Hitler, condemning his stance. One of the case studies in this book describes the Jewish uprising in the Warsaw ghetto as a kind of *satyagraha* in a desperate situation.

The wars of and against religious activism in the early twenty-first century can also be analyzed in a Gandhian way, in part because voices on both sides have stated their positions in moral terms. Yet, as in all fights, the moral elements are often overwhelmed by other factors: violence, political posturing, and self-serving efforts to promote particular leaders and privileged communities. These negative aspects are like clouds that limit the vision of each side, blinding it to a more creative solution than brute force can allow.

The prolonged conflict in Northern Ireland, taken as a case study in this book, shows how a situation of vicious terrorism can be brought to a peaceful end. As in all fights, the Gandhian task is to see beyond the destructive aspects of an encounter. When the religious claims are over territory—as in Northern Ireland or in Palestine—it is a matter of finding a way for opponents to begin to perceive themselves as cohabitants in a contested land. When the religious issue is ideological, it is often a matter of keeping the extremists from framing the issues their way and dictating how a conflict should be fought. Violence is seldom quelled by violence alone.

Even in extreme cases, there may be something to be gained by incorporating elements of an opponent's positions into one's own. Religious activists who challenge the secular state may provide at least one useful insight for society: the notion that the values of religion should help to animate the moral conscience of public life and give meaning to social identities in a global age. This message of morality and meaning may appear paradoxical, considering the strident manner in which it is sometimes conveyed.

Yet the Gandhian point is made. Even in dark moments one can glimpse the solutions that may eventually bridge positions that now seem so diverse and hostile as to be irreconcilable. Perhaps this, more than anything else about Gandhi's way of conflict resolution, indicates that it is worthy of consideration: in the most impossible of circumstances it provides a flicker of hope.

Santa Barbara
December 2004

SECTION I:
THE GANDHIAN FIGHT

❧ 1
Fighting a Gandhian Fight

In my opinion, the beauty and efficacy of satyagraha are so great and the doctrine so simple that it can be preached even to children.[1]

The basic idea of Gandhi's approach to fighting is to redirect the focus of a fight from persons to principles. Gandhi called it satyagraha, "grasping onto principles," or "truth force."[2]

He assumed that behind any struggle lies another clash, a deeper one: a confrontation between two views that are each in some measure true. Every fight, to Gandhi, was on some level a fight between differing "angles of vision" illuminating the same truth.[3]

This means that most of the ways that you and I fight simply miss the point. We either grapple with the person who represents a position or else try to accommodate that person, without struggling with the position itself. That, to Gandhi's mind, leaves the real conflict unresolved. It simmers in the background, ready to boil over on another occasion.

Let's take an example. Ms. A, let's say, is having a rather nasty chat with Mr. B. It could be any everyday conflict—a tension in their personal relationship or a battle over organizational policy. But in this case it's a backyard quarrel over where a fence should go. Ms. A thinks the line is on the far side of the tree that stands between her house and his, and Mr. B is convinced that the line is several feet back toward Ms. A's house, beside the rhododendron bushes. Because of an old surveying error, neither claim can be made with absolute certainty. Their conflict has all the ambiguities and charged emotions that fuel old feuds, and there are several possibilities for its outcome.

In this as in any conflict, the simplest resolution is *forced victory*.

Let's say that Ms. A seizes a moment when Mr. B is away and places the fence exactly where she wants it, securing the posts with poured concrete.

Mr. B returns to a *fait accompli*, and an uneasy calm prevails. The uneasiness is due to the fact that there has been no real resolution. What appears to be the end of the dispute may be just the opening in another chapter in the conflict. Like the legendary wars of Appalachian families, such endless skirmishes may be passed from generation to generation in a continuing blood feud. The issues underlying the tension remain, and each time one of the sides suffers a defeat the old conflict is compounded with a new one. The loser resents being bludgeoned into submission.

So instead of providing a real resolution, Ms. A's presumptuous fence may only set the stage for an even more vicious conflict to come. That battle, like many that you and I have fought, will be only the reappearance of an old fight, regardless of the pretext over which it may be waged. Like the wars that have plagued Europe in the past several centuries, the unneighborly hostilities of A and B may issue in repeated outbreaks of old conflicts that were never quite resolved.

But the factors contributing to the European wars were complicated. The conflict between A and B is apt to appear to its participants to be a much simpler affair. Ms. A, for instance, may be quite certain about which side is undeniably correct and which side is absolutely wrong. She knows exactly where the boundary line falls, and feels that the sheer obviousness of the truth of her claim is reason enough to justify her forced triumph over Mr. B.

This is fine enough if she is right. But what if she is wrong, even the tiniest bit wrong? Her measurements may be slightly off, her memory of the original line a bit faulty.

A look at history shows what can happen when large groups of people act with an unbending but unwarranted sense of certainty like hers. The very terms we use to refer to moral presumptuousness —a crusading attitude, an inquisitional style—remind us of those sad episodes when assaults were mounted with an absolute conviction of truth. Only later did history judge the zealots who undertook them to be seriously misguided.

It may appear that Gandhi also acted with an unswerving conviction that what he was doing was always right. And frequently his sense of resolve did border on what his adversaries, and even members of his own family, regarded as stubbornness. But this bullheadedness was tempered by an important Gandhian insight. This is the notion that even though one position may have more truth than another, each side has some portion of truth in its possession. This, it seems to me, is a basic premise of the Gandhian approach.

Stubborn though he may have been, Gandhi made a point of looking at both sides of issues. For example, even though he came to feel that British rule in India was not right for either the British or the Indians, he strongly defended what he felt to be the value of British civilization wherever it appeared. And, although he led the fight that threw the British out of India, he did not want to toss away the good things their presence had brought.

So Ms. A and Mr. B will have to look carefully at their conflict, and see if it isn't possible that both of them are at least partially right. Ms. A may remember that although the tree has always been on her side, it now bends slightly toward his. And Mr. B may recall that when the line went beside the rhododendrons, the rhododendrons were rambling in an odd direction, and anyway they were much smaller bushes then. The seeds of doubt in each of their minds indicate that perhaps there is something to be said for both sides.

I suspect that this is often so. Most of the arguments that you and I know are like this—not a matter of black and white, but of competing shades of gray. Even when one position initially appears to be faultlessly true, flaws are apt to emerge in its facade. If they do, the first option we are considering, the forced-victory solution, is doubly damaging: it fails to mend the underlying differences, but by appearing to do so, it masks the conflict that remains. For these reasons, the Gandhian logic regards it as fundamentally wrong.

Fortunately there are other ways these neighbors can resolve their conflict. If Ms. A and Mr. B are in a civil mood they might negotiate

their differences and come to a *compromise*. Mr. B, in a magnanimous gesture, might offer to forgo half of his demands if Ms. A will
agree to do the same. Perhaps he suggests a boundary line that
looks like the letter z. With it, each of them seems to win a little, and
the two can live together in a certain degree of harmony. There will
be no victims, and no one will harbor resentment over being forcibly
conquered.

Yet even though they both appear to win a little in their compromise, both lose a little as well. Both neighbors fail to get exactly
what they want. Even if Ms. A agrees to Mr. B's proposal, she may
never really accept his point of view. In her heart she knows where
the boundary line lies. She agrees to live with this zig-zag fence for
the sake of harmony, but the harmony that results is really only the
cessation of their verbal battle.

The uneasy quiet that results may be the best outcome they can
hope for—and a better ending than many that you or I have known
—but it still leaves them somewhat unsatisfied. The underlying conflict is still unresolved, and like the arrangement between Chamber-
lain and Hitler at Munich, their compromise could lead to disaster.
At some point in the future Mr. B could go digging for a sewer line
in what Ms. A still regards as her soil, and the two would be at each
other once again.

Compromise is not always a happy solution, and Gandhi seemed
ambivalent toward it. Sometimes he urged fighters to compromise,
and sometimes he discouraged them from doing so. When he dis-
dained compromise it was usually the kind of compromise I have
just been describing: accommodation. The other kind, to which he
was more favorably disposed, involved an agreement over principles, and I will come to that in a moment. But accommodation is
quite different from that. It involves only a superficial adjustment for
the sake of coexistence; when this type of compromise is relied on,
the lingering differences between opponents often remain. The tensions stay and fester. Sometimes they explode.

So it is good that Ms. A and Mr. B can choose still another means
to resolve their conflict. They can take their case to court and appeal
to the *law*. Ms. A, for instance, can hire a lawyer who will state her

side of the case eloquently before the bar, and Mr. B, if he is fortunate, will find one equally as talented. Ultimately a judge or a jury will make a decision based on what is considered an impartial body of legal precedent, a store of judgments applicable to everyone on an equal basis.

But is the law always so fair? Martin Luther King, Jr., was sent to the Birmingham jail precisely because he felt that certain laws were unjust. And a century earlier Thoreau was put behind bars because of a similar refusal to accept a legal code that he regarded as immoral. Gandhi read Thoreau when he was young, and like him went to jail willingly to protest unjust laws.

Gandhi also broke other laws—not because they were unjust but because they were minor regulations that were enforced with disproportionate severity to place obstacles in the path of a Gandhian campaign. Nuclear protestors in the United States and Europe have confronted similar legal hindrances. Many of the protestors have been arrested on charges of trespassing and disturbing the peace—laws they ordinarily would respect, but in times of necessity disobey.

At the same time that he broke the laws he considered unjust or unjustly applied, Gandhi professed great respect for the concept of law. He had been trained in London as an attorney, and had a high regard for the codes of propriety and morality that legal strictures represent. But he believed that beyond all laws lies the ultimate law, the law of God, and one must respect it before one can even consider breaking the lesser ones. "No man should become a law unto himself," he cautioned.[4]

Yet the lesser laws, the human ones, cannot always be relied on as resources for overcoming conflicts between opposing sets of principles. They are less helpful in judging which side is right than in judging which side is wrong; they are better at curing the symptoms of conflicts than assessing the cause of them; they cannot be easily adapted to the peculiarities of each situation; and they seldom allow for a judgment to which both sides can agree with equal satisfaction.

In the case of *Ms. A v. Mr. B,* for instance, resorting to the law might indeed prove that an old surveyor's error is at the heart of the problem. If that happened, it would be difficult for the court to rule precisely for one side or the other. A judgment in favor of Ms. A might leave Mr. B steaming mad. He might feel that the truthful aspects of his point of view were not acknowledged. From his perspective, he might feel that Ms. A reaped the same benefit that she would have if she had forced her victory by building her own version of the fence.

If the judge were in a more conciliatory mood, he or she could award a split decision to both A and B. But that might make both of them unhappy. They might each feel as wronged as the mother of the child King Solomon decided to divide. Such a decision, like those forged through an accommodation type of compromise, might allow for the worst of both worlds, rather than the best. A fence right down the middle of the neighbors' disputed land might anger both of them and, for that matter, obliterate the rhododendrons. Even at their most conciliatory, laws may not produce the sort of solution that will satisfy both plaintiffs and defendants all of the time.

But that, I believe, is precisely the goal of the Gandhian approach of *satyagraha:* to satisfy both parties to a conflict that their positions have been honored. In Gandhi's view, both Ms. A and Mr. B should win. The Gandhian approach holds out hope for a resolution that is better for each of them than if either one had forced a victory on the other.

How can this happen? First, Ms. A and Mr. B must stop attacking one another. Then they must abandon their narrow positions, and hunt for a resolution sufficiently broad that it can incorporate both sides at the same time.

Is this an impossible goal? One might wonder why anybody would abandon a position in an argument unless forced to do so. But Gandhi often did just that, claiming that it was more enriching to search for a broad solution than to defend a narrow one.

But there are other, more practical reasons for abandoning a position. Let's say that Ms. A and Mr. B simply become exhausted with the sheer effort of waging the fight. Their conflict, like many of yours and mine, begins to collapse on itself and becomes a protracted war in which both sides lose and lose and lose. In such stalemates both sides may crave a reconciliation more desperately than they desire to vindicate their old positions. Ms. A and Mr. B may wearily willingly abandon their old stances and join in a search for a mc harmonious alternative.

If they do so, they may be tempted to accept any settlement that presents itself, but the kind of alternative that would really please them (and Gandhi, for that matter) is an arrangement that would allow each side to gain as much as, or more than, it had bargained for in the first place. If this is to be the case, and both sides are to win, some sort of synthesis between their old positions is required. In creating it, the combatants will have to leave their old positions behind and come to a higher order of agreement.

In abandoning their old positions, Ms. A and Mr. B must put aside their claims to the disputed land, and with them the basis on which their claims are made: that each has the right to possess the land as his or her own private property. As they search for a broader area of agreement, they may consider several alternative bases for landownership, including the principle of shared property. If they come to agreement on that principle, then down comes the fence. The result may be a shared garden on the contested land.

This way of arriving at a solution is the Gandhian ideal, and it presents a cozy image. Both neighbor A and neighbor B are happier, we assume, than if either had won the battle outright, for each has now gained the resources of the other in the partnership. Ms. A has access to Mr. B's rake and hoe, and Mr. B can use Ms. A's garden hose.

Yet we can think of many reasons why the neighbors may not be pleased, and in other chapters we will look at these. For instance, even if we can imagine them happy with the solution over the land, what happens when it's time to pull the weeds? The Gandhian answer is the same that you or I might give: most likely, a new conflict will arise. If so, the process of working things out begins all over again.

This new Gandhian process would proceed in just the way that the one before did. In it, three steps were taken, steps one must take in any Gandhian fight. One must:

1) *examine the principles of both sides* to come to an agreement over which are valid and deserve to be a part of the solution;

2) create a Gandhian alternative to what presently exists by sorting through all imaginable options until finding a resolution that enhances both points of view;

3) begin doing the alternative, and discard any previous notions about how to win the fight for one's own side.

There are still a number of questions to be asked about this process: How do you know there *is* a Gandhian alternative? How can you tell when you have one? And what if you want to take the Gandhian approach but your opponent does not? If you have already raised these questions, bear with us. We will take them up as we go along. They are practical problems as well as theoretical concerns, and Gandhi had to deal with them all.

Ways of Resolving a Conflict

CONFLICT involves a clash between both persons and underlying principles.

FORCED VICTORY removes the person but the underlying conflict between principles remains.

ACCOMMODATION & COMPROMISE let each side win a little; but each side loses a little as well.

ARBITRATION & LAW judge which side is right-- but often neglect the truth in the loser's position.

SATYAGRAHA attempts to find a new position, more inclusive than the old ones, and moves into it.

♣ 2
Why Fight at All?

Inaction at a time of conflagration is inexcusable. [1]

You may have thought of another option in the fight between the quarreling neighbors—the option of not fighting at all. Mr. B might simply run off, or in some other way try to avoid the confrontation altogether.

Would that necessarily be such a bad thing? you might ask. Are there not some fights that are better left unfought?

No doubt there are. And Gandhi would not insist that you and I fight every one. In his own life he had to choose which encounters to take on. For one thing, he usually made a point of not getting involved in other people's fights. Although he sometimes acted as a mediator in labor disputes—once in an indigo plantation, and once in a textile mill—he ordinarily felt that only those persons who were directly involved in a conflict were in a position to resolve it.

Many of our own efforts at fighting are wasted on fights that we cannot win because these battles are not really ours to wage in the first place. Children of divorced parents, for instance, often grieve needlessly over their inability to patch up differences between their mothers and fathers, differences they had no direct role in creating. The bitterness of many Vietnam veterans comes from the feeling that they were sent to fight a war that they could not win because, they claim, it was never really America's to fight.

Some fights, of course, do genuinely affect us, but even some of these are better left unfought. If the issue in dispute is a petty one and is apt to distract us from more important matters, then it is best ignored. Especially dangerous are those instances in which members of a board or committee get so caught up in spats among themselves that they are unable to take on the business at hand. As a result of this squabbling, the organization—the school or church or business—may founder.

So there is no reason you or I should fight every fight that comes our way; Gandhi was quite clear on this point. But he recoiled against the notion that fear should ever be a factor in choosing which war to wage and which to abandon. If Ms. A is trying to decide whether the fight with Mr. B is worth fighting, the one factor she should not consider, according to Gandhi, is how nasty he can be, how difficult he could make the conflict. Such concerns have nothing to do with the merits of the fight. They do, however, affect our perception of it and may weaken our resolve. If these fears were to keep Ms. A from fighting, Gandhi would regard her as having failed to stand by her principles and having abandoned her conscience as well. Fighting, if it is nonviolent, is "never demoralizing," Gandhi claimed, whereas "cowardice always is."[2]

Another factor that we cannot let influence us is our ability to ignore the fight. If we are the ones oppressed, a conflict is difficult to ignore. If we are the stronger party, however, we are less tempted to deal with the fight. If Ms. A owns both sets of properties and Mr. B is her tenant, then she may feel that the boundary dispute is academic. She is in the position of being able to ignore B (thus stifling the dispute at the outset), even if the issue is important to his sense of space and security. From the Gandhian point of view, however, it would be wrong for her to do so. She would in effect be imposing a forced victory on the conflict before the fight has even had the chance to begin.

If cowardice and power should not keep us from a fight, what should propel us into one? How do we choose which fights are worth the effort of fighting? The ones Gandhi chose were those in which the issues at stake were fundamental: the rights of workers, the dignity of labor, a nation's freedom and its integrity. In Gandhi's case such issues were often found in grand encounters, but even simple spats can carry such freight. It may be, for example, that personality conflicts between members of a board of directors go far beyond matters of personal style, dress, or speech. These superficial traits may actually signal deep differences of orientation on policy questions, and the first task when friction emerges is to dig beneath the namecalling and find out whether the superficial does represent something more.

If there is an issue of principle lurking in the wings, the fight may be worth waging even if the matter in dispute is a small one. The task then is to see the conflict from the points of view of each of the combatants. You might find that one party is only interested in protecting his or her turf, whereas the other party has a genuine policy concern. If it were heard, it might favorably affect the whole direction of the organization. If you value the welfare of the whole group, you would jump in at this point and make sure that the hidden concern receives a real consideration. Or you might feel that one side has the greater weight of truth, and in that case you would openly defend it.

Gandhi claimed to enter many fights for just this reason—to side with those fighting for principle rather than for power or pride. It seems to me, however, that he entered many fights with another purpose in mind: not so much to defend the truth as to discover it. In fights like this, it would not be clear at the outset which side was right. Gandhi believed that the very process of fighting would bring into bold relief the truth and the deception of both sides.

The implications of this idea are enormous. If you take it seriously and are concerned about trying to find the right way out of a problem, then it means that you should not shirk a fight, but enter into it with enthusiasm. Fighting may be the only way you can tell what is right.

Though this is one of the most interesting aspects of the Gandhian approach, Gandhi himself never stated it quite so directly as I have here. What he said was that truth has many facets, that a good fight involves holding fast to the truth that you see, that a person's view of truth may change, and that underlying the different sides of a debate is a more fundamental conflict: "the eternal duel between the forces of darkness and light."[3]

The thread that ties these ideas together, I believe, is the notion that truth—the force of light—can emerge only in the process of fighting.

Perhaps an example will help explain how this can be so. Let's say that two workers in a delicatessen are having an awful time getting along with each other. One of them, a waitress, feels that the fellow who slices the cold cuts is sloppy in his work and overly social with the customers. And he, though he acknowledges that she is an efficient worker, sees her as a cold and ineffective representative of the store in dealing with the public.

What began as mutual mistrust has escalated to snide remarks and a distant attitude in their dealings with each other. At this point the situation is murky: strong feelings abound, but neither person has really analyzed what is wrong with the attitude of the other, although on the surface the faults of the other seem patently obvious. The deeper clarity—the unearthing of the principles that are at issue—can come only when each side challenges the other. Alas, this may happen in a less than friendly fashion.

On one particularly busy and unpleasant afternoon, the cold cut man's charming but bungling manner brings the waitress to the breaking point. In a moment of desperation, she calls him a gabby socializer. He in turn accuses her of being a cold fish, and threatens to hit her with one. The fight produces heat, but also some light, for in the ensuing conversation they pour out their feelings toward each other. Each one's work style undergoes the scrutiny that only an adversary can provide.

In the process of fighting, they may have to alter the views they have held of each other's position, and even of their own. The waitress may concede that her efficiency might apear to some customers as rudeness, and that her co-worker's sociability is a good thing for the store. From the other side, the cold cut man may admit that his ineptitude detracts from the cheer that he feels his pleasant demeanor brings to the deli. Her stand, which at first seemed to him totally wrong, may appear to have at least a grain of truth. And he may find that his own stance, though it initially seemed so splendid and selfless, was flawed with tiny falsehoods.

There is seldom very much moral clarity at the outset of any fight—even if that is precisely when the combatants feel surest of themselves. From a Gandhian point of view, that sense of certainty is a dangerous delusion, and the first moments of a fight may bring a rude awakening. Both parties may be forced to recognize that some of their previous claims are invalid.

Such fights can be therapeutic. Without one, the delicatessen workers might become increasingly sullen and disconsolate. But if they let their frustrations out in the open, the air can clear and attitudes can improve. The tensions that most of us experience in the course of any given day may be hints of fights that never get fought. If they are not allowed to surface we may have to deal with them later on in an even more strident form. Sometimes marriages in which the partners "never fight" are followed by the bitterest of divorce suits.

Gandhi's view of conflict and the importance of expressing it is one of his most significant insights, and he found it confirmed in the teachings of the *Bhagavad Gita,* a Hindu scripture. According to his interpretation, the *Gita* regards each person as possessing truth and untruth together: "The field of battle is in our own body,"[4] Gandhi said, summarizing its teachings.

The logical extension of this way of thinking is the notion that conflict is the crucible in which the two can be separated out; truth can be forged and untruth burned away. This may be the reason why Gandhi sometimes seemed to seek out fights. He may have wished to purify his moral stand through the challenges that conflict offers.

Now you may feel that such high expectations about fighting are not warranted. The clashes that we know are often full of nasty cracks and underhanded jabs. They deserve little optimism: the fighters fight dirty, they hide more than they reveal, and their minds are often closed.

These kinds of battles are a long way from serving as textbook cases of moral clarification. Yet the problem, Gandhi might claim, is not the fights, but us: we do not expect enough from them, or take the care to wage them creatively. You will have to admit that when someone calls you a nasty name, your first impulse is not to think of the opportunities for moral insight that such a confrontation offers. It takes a great deal of effort to make a fight a positive rather than a negative affair, and one has to master the skills involved. To Gandhi, fighting was an art that had to be learned, and he stressed that nonviolent fighting in particular required "training of a different kind."[5]

So it is good to learn how to fight effectively and creatively. But even if we do not—even if we fight the ordinary, dirty way—our fighting may still be useful. It may bring submerged conflicts into the open and allow us to be aware of hidden points of view. If you and I weren't criticized or even upbraided from time to time, we might suffer from the illusion that we are universally appreciated, and find ourselves entranced by an improbably admirable self-portrait. Such views might lead us into unpleasant clashes with reality farther down the road.

Even an unending, seemingly hopeless battle may have a hidden potential, for the very fact that a stalemate exists may cause the fighters to look for an alternative to their mired, defensive positions. Often it is only when we are exhausted from fight after fight that we begin to look for a less violent solution to our problems.

If you can believe that fighting and the search for a peaceful solution can be compatible, then you stand at the doorway to *satyagraha*, the approach to confrontation that encourages one to engage in conflict in order to find a solution to it. But before we take on *satyagraha*, we have to wrestle with the central concept on which it is based—Gandhi's notion of truth—for without it we have no way of knowing which solution to look for.

❧ 3

How Do You Know
When You're Right?

What may appear as truth to one person will often appear as untruth to another person. But that need not worry the seeker.[1]

Truth is a word often burdened with a great weight of simplistic moralism, and it might be nice if we could avoid it in discussing Gandhi's approach to peaceful fighting. Much as we might want to do that, however, we haven't the option. Gandhi's term for this sort of fighting, *satyagraha*, begins with the word *truth*.

The term is pronounced "sut-*yah*-gruh-huh," with a slightly greater emphasis on the second syllable than the others. It was coined by Gandhi to describe the process of looking for the truthful aspects of each side's position, trying to find a broad resolution that includes them all, and clinging to it.

How do you know which aspects are more truthful than others? How do you know a truthful resolution when you see it? And how, for that matter, do you know that there really is a truthful resolution to be had? The last question is the most fundamental, and it is the one with which we shall begin.

The answer can be found in the word itself. The term Gandhi uses for truth, *satya*, is based on the Sanskrit verb meaning *to be*. It implies a connection between truth and existence. Truth, in this sense, is what is.[2]

Most of us can accept this notion of truth with regard to the physical world: truth in the scientific sense is verified by observable reality. But what if our eyes deceive us, or if the reality is too little or big, too microscopic or too cosmic, to behold? We are then forced to accept as truth the regular patterns that can be discerned through mathematical conclusions or logical deductions. When we cannot observe what is, logic can convince us that it is there, a hidden stratum of reality beneath the observable world. Quarks and neurons, for example, were discovered through scientific logic before they were observed in the laboratory.

That's fine for physics, you may say. But what does this have to do with the world of choice and conflict?

Gandhi believed there was a connection. He claimed that like the natural order, the realm of human values contains a level of truth deeper than what meets the eye. For him, moral reality was as certain as physical reality: there is "truth in thought, truth in speech, truth in action."³ He employed science as a metaphor for moral knowledge. Just as there are laws of nature, reasoned Gandhi, there are laws of harmonious living. Our task is to seek them out, to "experiment with truth"⁴ the way a scientist might use a laboratory. There was no doubt in Gandhi's mind that eventually one could find the right way to act in any situation.

Moral reality is not so obvious as physical reality, and for many of us even to accept the existence of such a thing is largely an act of faith. Gandhi himself implicitly conceded the point. He often spoke of truth in a religious sense: "Truth," he stated, "is God."⁵ For him the reverse was equally valid: all of God and religion could be summed up as a search for truth.

Many of us immediately assent to this way of thinking, but others of us are not such ready believers. Gandhi's conception of religion and truth may seem too much to take. Do I have to believe in this sort of moral reality, you may ask, to make any sense of Gandhi?

His answer would be yes, for the notion of *satyagraha* is rooted in it. But before you part company with Gandhi forever over this issue, you should know that by his standards you may be more moral than you think. Consider how you would answer these questions:

• Do you believe in human rights? If so, you are affirming a belief in a higher moral order and accepting a conviction of Western thought that parallels Gandhi's insistence on the dignity of all life.

• Do you chafe at moral relativism, the notion that morality changes from one situation to another? If so, you would agree with Gandhi and most Hindus that some moral truths endure.

• Are you concerned about doing the right thing even when you don't have to? Then like Gandhi you have internalized your moral standards, and made them part of your life.

• Do you resist following moral rules you don't agree with? If so, it may be because your idea of morality, like Gandhi's, is linked with the quality of life rather than with rules or regulations. Like him, you may need to know *why* you should do something right, not just *what* you are supposed to do.

In fact, Gandhi made a habit of challenging conventional morality more than most of us do. Even though he believed that there is a higher morality, he claimed no perfect knowledge of it, and regarded all the usual wisdom about what is right and wrong as something that needed to be continually reexamined. "True morality," Gandhi argued, could not be found in "following the beaten track."[6] A good Gandhian fight, then, calls into question the truthfulness of every position, no matter how vaunted.

Gandhi thought that moral truth, like the secrets of the physical universe, had been glimpsed only distantly and were only partially codified. All the existing moral and legal codes, he felt, mirror the ultimate order in less than perfect ways. No one of them is intrinsically more sacred than the others. Truth is wherever you find it.

That leads us back to the questions with which we began this section: where do we find truth, and how do we know it when we see it?

Again, the Sanskrit word for truth gives a clue to the answer. *Satya* is derived from *sat*, the verb denoting existence, the *is* verb; and this implies that the most fundamental truth is existence itself.

That which exists, lives. Something truthful, therefore, is life-affirming, and a Gandhian respect for truth leads to an attitude of "good will towards all life."[7]

Let us consider how this might help the quarrelling neighbors, Ms. A and Mr. B, decide which of them is right. We have already determined that the first thing Ms. A and Mr. B need to do is to look for

Steps in the Process of Satyagraha

the truthful aspects of their own positions. We can now define those aspects as the things that defend life, enhance life, allow life to flourish, and bring lives together in harmony.

At the same time A and B need to toss out the untruthful aspects of their positions. These are those things that inhibit, denigrate, and destroy life, and alienate one life from another.

You may not find these definitions of truth and untruth to be very specific. Alas, it may not be possible to make them more so. Gandhi did not write about truth in any detail—not even with as much specificity as I have given here. Rather, he provided a basic stance for gauging truth, an attitude applicable to a wide range of circumstances. This attitude he called nonviolence: "not just harmlessness but a positive state"[8] that allows those who adopt it to disentangle life-affirming traits from destructive ones. Sorting out truth from falsehood is arduous work, and is much of what a Gandhian fight is about.

Since this task is based on an attitude rather than precise rules, it may appear to be a subjective matter. At one point, Gandhi seemed to say as much. When a British committee of inquiry asked him about his concept of truth, and demanded to know who would have the right to determine it, Gandhi answered, "The individual himself." But in any fight there is more than one individual involved, presumably each with different views of where the truth lies. Wouldn't that, the British official wanted to know, surely lead to confusion? Gandhi's reply was enigmatic: "I do not think so."[9]

It seems an odd reply because the heat of most fights—as Gandhi was surely aware—comes precisely from the confusion over where and on whose side the truth lies. Ms. A and Mr. B cannot both be completely right, even when they think they are. So truth is always a relative judgment. Yet, as we have seen, their views can both be *partially* true. The reason for this, according to Gandhi, is that both views are based on one absolute idea of truth. This truth is as ineffable as it is absolute, however, and our perception of it is always truth with a small *t*, a proximate vision. Our version of truth is the best we can have, but because it is not Truth with a capital *T* it can always be challenged and changed. So another person's view of truth need not lead to confusion, as Gandhi said, but to the possibility of improving our own view.

Fortunately, in many instances the truthful, life-affirming choice becomes obvious to all. The choice between giving one's money to the needy or buying some useless extravagance, for example, should not ordinarily require a great deal of moral reflection.

In other cases even Gandhi might admit that the right choice is not so quickly at hand— as when the purchase of something that may seem opulent, such as a new car, may lead to greater freedom and opportunities for social service. Either choice—to buy the car or not to buy it—entails a mixture of truth and deception. The object then is to avoid either of these choices, and find some way of retaining the positive aspects of both while discarding the negative in each: purchasing a second-hand vehicle for less money, for instance. By transcending the need to choose between the original options, we've moved closer to the Truth.

In the case of the quarreling neighbors, A and B, we might put their mutual desire to nurture the disputed land on the life-affirming side of the moral ledger, but their desire to possess it on the destructive side. The resolution is close at hand: by sharing the land and creating a garden, they can retain their nurturing tendencies and discard the possessive ones.

In this case, as in all Gandhian fights, the resolution is to be found in the situation itself. Both sides felt responsible for the land and wanted to do something creative with it. But they did not realize that their responsibility could be shared and their creativity enhanced if they worked together. The truthful elements were waiting to be uncovered and pieced together to form a whole.

Once you have decided that a certain solution to a conflict meets the criterion of truthfulness, then you are under an obligation to hold onto it, and to fight for it. Yet the troubling thing about Gandhi's notion of truth is that you never have the luxury of knowing for certain that you are right, even though you may feel that you are. Even though you devote most of your energies in a fight towards having your version of the truth accepted as the rightful one, Gandhi would have you retain some interest in continuing to

FIRST all the aspects
of each side's
position are articulat[...]

A's list
1. Desire to possess the land.
2. Sense of responsibility for the land.
3. Feeling of power in getting B to grovel in submission.
4. Desire to have a garden.
5. Desire for civility and neighborliness.

B's list
1. Desire to possess the land.
2. Feeling of power in having a fence.
3. Sense of responsibility for the land.
4. Desire to have a garden.

THEN the lists are compared.

The arrows show areas of agreement.

The crossed-out items are those deemed to be self-serving, destructive and untruthful.

The circled items are those seen as positive & truthful, and conducive to harmony.

(Those neither circled nor crossed-out are yet to be determined.)

3 NOW a resolution can be formed, beginning with those truthful aspects both sides share, and adding to them those truthful aspects brought to the conflict by only one of the sides.

A's list
1.
2.
3. Feeling of power in getting B to grovel.
4.

B's list
1. Desire to possess the land.
2. Feeling fear of having in a fence
3.

A & B's list

sense of responsibility for the land.

sense of responsibility for the land.

desire to have a garden.

civility and neighborliness

The "yet-to-be-determined" items may be added to the resolution as experiments. If they are helpful in bringing harmony they are kept. If not, they may be discarded.

✗ (joint) possession of the land. ?

look for an even more truthful answer. Thus you must not only fight for what you think is right, you must fight with it. Even if Ms. A finds an old deed in her attic proving her legal right to the land, she might still be persuaded that Mr. B possesses a stronger moral claim than she does—especially if he demonstrates how much better off they would both be if they shared the gardening.

It is possible that even at the very end of a struggle, Gandhian fighters may see that their version of truth has been limited all along, and may then switch to a different position. In one of Gandhi's own political campaigns, he claimed that his "interpretation [was] found to be incorrect." In order to "mend the error" he had to "start the movement over again."[10]

As vexing as it may seem, some would say that this open-ended quality in Gandhi's understanding of truth is just what saves it from the rigidity of moralism. Satyagraha does not offer certainty. It provides the license to hunt for truth, not a certificate that it is in hand.

❀ 4
Violence: The Breakdown of a Fight

One single act of violence . . . would have lost their cause.[1]

Gandhi has so often been identified with the notion of nonviolence that up to this point in our discussion I have scarcely needed to mention the term. Yet the idea is not as self-evident as it may appear. Even those who know that Gandhi favored nonviolence may not know why he did so, or why it was so central to his approach.

Nonviolence, according to Gandhi, is the litmus test of truth. When Ms. A and Mr. B were puzzling over their options and trying to decide which solution to choose to resolve their small quarrel, Gandhi might have guided them with this advice: if it involves violence, throw it out.

The reason for this is that in Gandhi's lexicon, violence is very close to being the same thing as untruth. It stands for all the same traits—the obstructive, destructive, life-negating, alienating tendencies—that one finds in the camp opposite from truthfulness. The term that Gandhi used for violence, *himsa,* is a Sanskrit word that means "the desire to harm."[2] By extension, then, Gandhi used *himsa* to describe anything that violates—in a physical, mental or emotional way—the integrity of something living. And he meant for it to include the very attitude of wanting that violence to come about, hurting other people "by every evil thought."[3]

Ahimsa, "nonviolence," is therefore much more than the absence of destruction. It is the absence of the *desire* to destroy. Or put in more positive terms, it is the presence of the desire to nurture, and

Gandhi often compared it with the Christian notion of self-giving love.

In the context of conflict, *ahimsa* means not harming your opponents, not wanting to harm them, and being concerned about their welfare. Like Jesus' injunction to love your enemy and "turn the other cheek," Gandhi's advice was to "do good even to the evildoer."[4] Gandhi would have been moved by the way in which Martin Luther King, Jr., and his freedom fighters in Alabama refused to counter violence with violence, even when they were beaten and attacked by guard dogs. He would have been even more impressed by the way in which King's followers prayed for those who abused them.

Being nonviolent, therefore, is more than just a matter of not striking back. And violence is more than the simple use of physical strength. Gandhi's enlarged definition of the term includes any sort of coercion, be it physical, verbal, or emotional, and he decries even the *intent* to coerce. Judged by this standard, many of us fight violently even though we are civil when we do so.

In fact, according to Gandhian thought, most fights we know are violent. They are violent not only when one side pummels the other, but when it employs schemes of manipulation behind closed doors. Mr. B is violent if he threatens to blackmail Ms. A, and she is violent if she retaliates by tricking him into submission.

You may agree with Gandhi that these are violent scenes, and familiar ones at that. In fact, these images may be your picture of what conflict is all about. It is hard to imagine a fight without them. We might understand why someone who dislikes such brutalities would avoid a fight, but it is more difficult to understand why someone like Gandhi who likes to fight would refuse to resort to manipulation and physical force. Why did he consider these tactics useless?

The answer is simple: violence negates life. Pummeling, scheming, blackmailing, tricking—none of these things is conducive to a search for truth; none of these affirms life.

These acts are destructive even if they do not physically destroy, for in Gandhi's view coercion and violence are virtually the same. If you coerce, you destroy the will and freedom of other person, and that, he reasoned, is as harmful as hurting the body. Gandhi said that any tactic that employs coercion "ceases to be moral."[5]

When coercion inhibits the freedom of one of the fighters, it inhibits the freedom of the fight. The Gandhian fight involves a give and take between opponents. In that free-for-all of ideas, an alternative to the conflict will appear, one that both sides can agree on and affirm.

A person cannot think reflectively with a gun at the head. If a boss gives her subordinate ten minutes to either agree to a policy position or be fired, it is doubtful that the subordinate will offer creative alternatives to her position. They should come to terms with each other's ideas on their own, without pressure. According to Gandhi, if we are searching for truth we must "guarantee to our opponents the same freedom we claim for ourselves."[6] Coercion short-circuits the process of searching for a solution; as soon as coercion enters, openness is gone.

Coercion is harmful, but Gandhi did not regard all forms of force as coercive, and we should not imagine his approach as being purely pleasant and quiescent. He employed many pressure tactics—strikes, boycotts, demonstrations, and other forms of noncooperation—but he claimed that he used them only to bring an issue forcefully to an opponent's attention. It is on such tactics that a Gandhian fighter should rely. An opponent may be abnormally dull, obstinate and thick-skinned, for instance, and it may require a lot of noise and shaking to gain his or her attention. But such measures are not necessarily coercive. Coercion applies only to tactics that are used to force an opponent beyond his or her will, and leave that opponent no choice but to capitulate.

This kind of coercion is forbidden even when the Gandhian fighters are convinced that the whole truth is on their side. As we have seen before, that is never quite the case, for even the most unscrupulous fighters still retain one trump card: their right to live, and to do so unharmed and with dignity. Since coercion violates that right, it always creates untruth, even when it is enlisted for a noble purpose.

From a Gandhian point of view, the use of coercion is not just fighting dirty, it is not fighting at all. If we use brute force, Gandhi said, "it means that we want our opponent to do by force that which we desire but he does not, and if such a use of force by us is justifiable, surely he is entitled to do likewise." In that event, Gandhi thought, "we should never come to an agreement. We may simply fancy, like the blind horse moving in a circle round a mill, that we are making progress."[7]

But you may have thought of special cases. If you are involved in a basically nonviolent struggle and need only a touch of coercion to pull through to victory at the last moment, wouldn't it be justified? Or if your side has disavowed the use of coercion but the other side has not, is the fight still a valid fight?

These questions have different answers.

With regard to the first, the matter of whether a little coercion can be mixed in with *satyagraha,* the answer is no. According to Gandhian theory, no amount of coercion can ever be condoned. Gandhi once prohibited his followers from even saying "shame, shame" to persuade people to adopt his way.[8] Any use of coercion, then, signals that the normal course of *satyagraha* has been abandoned.

The reason for this is that violent tactics counteract and disable nonviolent ones, and ultimately discredit the whole truth-searching process. If the Russian and American governments are busily testing new nuclear weapons at the same time they are negotiating limitations on old ones, it casts doubt on both sides' sincerity. And if our friends, A and B, spice their exchanges with manipulative words—or worse, if they threaten each other with lawsuits at each difficult juncture of the dispute—it is unlikely they will establish the fragile bond of trust that is essential to the Gandhian approach. In fact, any attempts at *satyagraha* by A in such a situation would probably be regarded by B as some sort of mischief, a ploy.

What if Ms. A refuses to succumb to the temptation to be coercive, but her opponent, Mr. B, shows no such restraint? Can she still conduct *satyagraha?*

The answer to this second question is somewhat different from the answer to the first. Regardless of what her opponent does, as long as she is following the Gandhian rules, Ms. A is still engaged in *satyagraha*. Her task of searching for a truthful resolution is definitely complicated, however, by the problem of trying to get B to come around, abandon his coercive tactics, and join her in a search for a Gandhian alternative.

Many conflicts in which you and I have been involved are of this difficult sort, in which only one side—somehow it seems always to be our own—is interested in playing fair. It is difficult to imagine *satyagraha* in such cases—so difficult, you may feel, as to be impossible. If B has armed himself to the teeth and is ready to adopt coercive measures, could he be persuaded to abandon them by someone who is not so armed or so eager? He has the ability to create fear, after all, and it seems unlikely that he could easily be talked into jettisoning this source of strength without some indication that it would be to his advantage to do so.

In fact this is just what Gandhi tried to do when faced with similar opponents—convince them that his viewpoint was valid for their side as well as for his own. In a labor dispute on an indigo plantation, for instance, Gandhi had been ordered by the court to leave the area, but he was able to convince the authorities that their purposes were better served not by opposing his investigation of unjust labor conditions, but by joining him. The district magistrate had accepted the plantation owners' assertion that there were no wrongdoings to be uncovered. But when Gandhi's investigation demonstrated the contrary, the judge professed embarrassment that he had not found these matters on his own, and he supported Gandhi's inquiry.

If Ms. A is trying to wage a Gandhian fight she will have to do what Gandhi did: demonstrate to Mr. B how sensible her approach to the problem is, even from his point of view. And we shall see how she could try to do just that. But one thing is always forbidden. Even in the face of violent force, she is not allowed to use that sort of force in return, or else the fundamental fight, the fight for principles, will be lost.

When a Gandhian stands for nonviolence, he or she also stands for that primal principle of truth, the affirmation of life itself. Those who take a nonviolent stand witness to that, even if no other point comes across to the opposing side. For that reason, Gandhian fighters have no reason to abandon a struggle out of fear that their opponents may use violence against them. The only violence they have to fear is their own.

❧ 5
What to Do with a Recalcitrant Opponent

An opponent is not always bad simply because he opposes.[1]

There may have been times when you have faced an opponent even more troubling than one who fights dirty—one who refuses to fight at all. Such a person may at first staunchly refuse to respond or to communicate with you, and then later, after he or she has built up a massive store of resentment, lash out in a vicious attack.

These moments are among the most difficult in a fight, and unfortunately they are very common. Sometimes those to whom we are closest—an old friend or a close co-worker—will hesitate to respond if they are unwilling or afraid to fight. More frequently, however, it is proud and distant opponents who close themselves off and refuse to take us seriously. Large organizations often seem to be like that, as do some people who are in positions of power much greater than our own.

Gandhi had to fight just such foes. The civility of the British in their response to the Indian movement for independence is highly overrated by those who feel that Gandhi's opponents were an easy mark for the nonviolent method. When Gandhi began his campaigns, the British officials were cold, inflexible and uninterested in conversation with that "naked fakir," as Churchill once called him. When the British did respond their messages were terse, negative, and sometimes accompanied by military force. The British rule was even capable of mass murder, as in the massacre at Amritsar in 1919.

So Gandhi's adversaries were not always such gentle folk, and some of our own opponents also can be inflexible, intransigent, and even ruthless. The quarrelling neighbors we have been observing in this book—basically decent people—have scarcely prepared us for this sort of opposition. All they needed was a little encouragement, and off they went down the nonviolent path.

But let's imagine that mild-mannered neighbor B has moved out. A new neighbor, Mr. C, moves in, and Ms. A watches him with mounting apprehension. He's a cantankerous old crank, that C, and doesn't mind anyone saying so. He quickly takes over Mr. B's side of the argument and defends it with a stolid intransigence. What is the hapless neighbor A to do?

The stage is set for a dreadful encounter. The question that disturbs Ms. A when she confronts this nasty new neighbor is the same one that any of us might raise in a similar conflict: when the opponent is cranky, suspicious, recalcitrant, what can we do?

Fight, Gandhi would answer, in the same way as if the opponent were pleasant, generous, and flexible. As we have observed in the previous chapter, a Gandhian is constrained to follow *satyagraha* regardless of the intentions of the opponent. Just because the opponent is uninterested in searching for a truthful resolution, this need not hinder the Gandhian from looking for one alone.

Gandhi's answer is not easy, and fortunately it is not the last word. He would also say that although the rules are fundamentally the same regardless of the enemy and the way he or she fights, the way they are applied may differ substantially depending on the situation.

The approach needs to be adjusted in situations when the opponents are dogged and unyielding, for instance. In such cases Gandhians are saddled with a dual responsibility. At the same time that they are trying to search for a truthful alternative, they have to try to involve their opponents in the fight. And while they are trying to engage their opponents and challenge them, they are trying to push on toward the Gandhian goal of a truthful alternative without unduly alienating their foes. They are trying not to "condemn but convert," to use Gandhi's words.[2] And at these times Gandhian fighters are walking a tightrope.

Take the case of poor A with her new neighbor. The initial step in the *satyagraha* process is to separate out the truthful and untruthful postures on each side of the dispute, and she may have to do it on her own. Neighbor C may show no interest in the procedure at all. Perhaps the only way she can involve him is to apprise him of what she is doing and hope that he will take interest in the process and join in.

It is important that she let him know what she is doing because in addition to conducting *satyagraha*, she is trying to convince her opponent that the fight is worth his effort. In order for him to acknowledge that, Mr. C will have to know that Ms. A is not only fighting for her own side—as an ordinary fighter might do—but that she has his welfare in mind as well. Such a realization may pique his interest: why, he may ask, would she want to defend him? Curiosity may propel him into the debate.

But maybe not. His curiosity may stay unmoved, and his response to Ms. A's friendly discussion of the divergence between their points of view may be nothing more than a snarl.

He may remain incommunicative even when Ms. A puts together the truthful aspects of both their positions in a proposal for a resolution to the conflict. Again, she must let Mr. C know what she is up to, what kind of Gandhian alternative she has formulated, and how it will benefit him. Again there may be silence from his side.

At this point Ms. A will have to make a decision. She has to decide whether she will wait until Mr. C joins her, or whether she will try to create the alternative alone. The first option would require her to mount a campaign to bring C to her side; the second would allow her to proceed as if her neighbor had already agreed.

Let's say she chooses the second option and tries to make the solution work on her own. As we soon shall see, she may be quickly thrust back to the first option, that of mounting a campaign to win Mr. C over. But at this point she is optimistic. She hopes that if Mr. C sees how interesting and mutually beneficial her solution is, he—

like Gandhi's adversaries in the indigo plantation labor dispute—will quickly embrace it.

So she begins. Let's say the solution she chooses is the same one we discussed before, when amiable Mr. B was her neighbor. She tries to turn the disputed land into a common garden. The unpleasant Mr. C glowers a bit, but she ignores his stares and begins buying seeds and planting fruit trees and acting as if the conflict were over.

It is possible that neighbor C might immediately see the virtues of neighbor A's solution and rush to join her in her display of horticultural zeal. But then, maybe not. Perhaps he might simply tolerate the whole affair, cloaking his distaste in heavy silence. At one level this would make things easy enough for neighbor A. But if she were truly attempting a Gandhian fight, she would not be satisfied with that. She would have to continue the struggle to mend the underlying differences on her own.

But things could be worse. What if neighbor C is neither so enthusiastic as the first response suggests nor so indifferent as the second implies? What if he builds a fence around the disputed area, keeps neighbor A and her fruit trees out, and threatens her with a shovel? Then she is faced with having to adopt the other task—launching a campaign to get him to reverse his mood—at the same time that she continues to try to create the garden.

What Ms. A does from here on is largely up to her imagination; there are no set tactics for a Gandhian fight. But there are constraints: she is not allowed to harm Mr. C, for instance, or treat him as the unyielding boor he appears to be. Gandhi would "resolutely refuse" to allow her—or us—"to consider opponents as enemies."[3] She is not allowed to do anything that would close off communication, or so limit her options that she could not change direction if necessary.

But she is allowed—in fact Gandhi would require her—to keep the issue alive. She is also obligated to let Mr. C know exactly what she thinks of his actions, and how she feels their fight could be resolved. And Gandhi would have her express this as forcefully as possible. He claimed that his prohibition against "the vilification of the opponent" did not exclude "a truthful characterization of his acts."[4] Gandhi would certainly approve if Ms. A wanted to express to Mr. C her "truthful characterization" of his hostile activities. She might begin by writings letters to him, and she might even mobilize the support of the local garden society to help her do so. In extreme frustration, she might even picket his house in order to drive her truthful characterization home.

But wait: these last two measures may sound to you more like coercion than nonviolence. Would Gandhi defend them?

He might. To Gandhi, the issue would be whether the measures are coercive, or whether they are merely dramatic and forceful ways of making a point. As we have seen, Gandhi prized freedom of choice. He said that "no action which is not voluntary can be called moral."[5] The question, then, is whether Mr. C is allowed to make choices in the struggle out of his own free will. If he has no room for independent action and can only acquiesce, then *satyagraha* has gone astray.

Let's say that this is not the case. Mr. C is quite free to throw away the letters from the garden society if he pleases. He is equally able to close his blinds to the scene of Ms. A parading with her picket signs in front of his lawn. Gandhi's view, then, would be that the battle is still on and it is still a fair fight.

It may seem easy enough to arrive at this conclusion in this case, but not all situations are so clear. What if Mr. C perceived himself as barricaded in his house by the very same actions that Ms. A regarded as being civil and mild? Gandhi's own campaigns were sometimes perceived as coercive, and faulted as such, though Gandhi usually denied the charge. It is occasionally a tricky matter to determine whether a tactic is coercive, and we will want to return to this issue later. For now, however, the point is this: recalcitrant opponents need not deter Gandhian fighters from waging Gandhian fights. But the opponents will require compassion from their Gandhian adversaries, and the fights will demand a great deal of ingenuity if they are to be waged both forcefully and nonviolently at the same time.

6
The Weapon:
The Goal Itself

If we take care of the means, sooner or later we are bound to reach the ends.[1]

The Gandhian way of fighting seems to present a dilemma. Even while you are in the midst of trying to fend off a persistent opponent, you are expected to tend to the differences of principle that lie beneath the conflict. Both tasks command your attention, and they seem to point you in opposite directions. It is difficult for Ms. A to search for a solution to her disagreement with the cantankerous Mr. C and at the same time try to prevent him from levelling her with his shovel. Which task, you may wonder, should she—and you—attend to first?

The Gandhian approach would have you avoid making this choice, and circumvent the dilemma in an ingenious way: by making the truthful alternative the method of resisting your opponent. If your opponent has not totally limited your options, then you can fight in the most direct way a Gandhian can: you can simply start carrying out your alternative to the conflict as if you had already won the right to do so.

Gandhi himself did this on several occasions while spearheading India's struggle for independence from the British. The truth for which Gandhi saw himself fighting was not just a state of political independence, but a self-reliance to undergird that independence. He wanted India not only to sever its colonial ties, but also to bolster its own internal economic and political system. The British, needless to say, wanted India to do neither.

One manifestation of the British control over the Indian economy was the system of taxation. A heavy tax was imposed by the British on even the most basic of commodities, such as salt. Gandhi protested this system, and in a letter to the British viceroy claimed that the tax on salt seemed to be "designed to crush the very life" out of the average Indian.[2] So one remarkable day Gandhi marched to the sea, accompanied by tens of thousands of followers, and began collecting the salt himself, despite a government interdiction.

In another expression of the same determination, he urged his compatriots to boycott British textile imports by developing a cottage industry based on the family spinning wheel. Gandhi encouraged them to throw away their British-made clothes—consign them to the flames—and "make the spinning wheel not only a symbol of simplicity and economic freedom, but also a symbol of peace."[3] The spinning wheel became so powerful a symbol, in fact, that the Congress party adopted it as an insignia. And the wheel that is now enshrined at the center of India's national flag carries more than one meaning: it is an ancient symbol of righteous rule and a reminder of Gandhi's defiant spinning wheel.

In these cases—Gandhi's salt march and his use of the spinning wheel as a method of protest—the means and the ends were the same. There was an "inviolable connection," Gandhi said, "between them."[4] Economic independence, as exemplified in the production of salt and textiles free from British taxes and industrial monopolies, was exactly the sort of thing he thought an independent, self-reliant nation should be about. So Gandhi and his compatriots began carrying out that goal, and the very act of doing it became a prime weapon in their struggle to resist the British. The goal was the means.

But Gandhi took this equation and used it in the opposite way as well, treating the means as the goal. By using nonviolence in his strategy for social change Gandhi hoped to ensure that the new Indian society to emerge from the struggle would be nonviolent too. If you attempt to use violent means to achieve a peaceful end, Gandhi argued, you will fail. You cannot justify destroying a country in order to save it. Gandhi thought that the purest goals could "never justify impure or violent action."[5]

Actions are habitforming. If you use coercion once, you increase the likelihood that you will use it again, and with every coercive act you build up a store of ill will in your opponent that decreases the possibility of a genuine resolution. Harmony, in such cases, recedes farther and farther from sight.

When Gandhi said "as the means, so the ends,"[6] he meant this dictum not just as a prescription to tailor your methods to your goals but as a statement of fact. To him it was clear that what you get out of a struggle depends upon what you put into it. He felt that the great failure of socialism in the Soviet Union stemmed from a choice Soviet leaders made early on. In using an army to vault their new regime to power, the Communists installed a military dictatorship that imposed itself on the Russian people. The lesson to be learned from the Soviet experience, thought Gandhi, was this: if you use violence as a strategy for political change, you end up with a political order based on violence. If you do not want that, then you have to plan your strategy for change differently.

Take the quarrel between Ms. A and her neighbor. She could build a fence, and that would be her means of staking claim to the disputed territory. But then that fence would become a part of the outcome, a permanent addition to the landscape. If she dreads the sight of fences the victory would be a hollow one. Even though it might be less effective in controlling Mr. C, creating a garden would be more effective in moving her toward the goal—especially, of course, if a garden is precisely the goal she has in mind. And the very act of creating the garden would be her method of protesting Mr. C's ideas of what to do with the disputed space.

So it seems Ms. A is going to have to think about her method of getting her way as well as the outcome she would like to achieve. Her means will affect her ends. If one of her long-range goals for living with her neighbor is a cordial, reasonable, and open relationship, then she should prepare the ground by adopting these traits at the very outset of the dispute. She should employ her end as a means, in order for the means to become the end.

Trying to find the correct means for fighting—not just formulating the correct goals—became increasingly important to Gandhi during his later years. Especially in the last fifteen years of his life, when he was relieved of the day-to-day pressures of political leadership, Gandhi focused on activities that would lead away from "impure or violent action"[7] and produce life-affirming goals as a natural consequence.

This focus of Gandhi's may be helpful to remember on those occasions when we are in the heat of a fight and a truthful solution does not seem easily at hand. The purity of the fighting should then be our immediate goal. For if the fight is waged nonviolently and openly and in a life-affirming way, in time the truthful options will emerge.

For that reason a goal is not always necessary. In fact, sometimes a goal—even a proximate, temporary one—might even get in the way. If Ms. A is obsessed with a garden as the only valid solution to the conflict, she may close her mind to an even more interesting possibility for using that small piece of land. If she were genuinely open to Mr. C's ideas and encouraged him to formulate a solution of his own, he might come up with one that would go beyond her own idea of a garden. He might want to plant a row of apple trees, for instance. The trees would provide him with a demarcation of territory and at the same time give her greenery and vegetables. So her own aims would be achieved, but in a way she had not quite envisioned herself. And her exposure to this new possibility would have come through being willing to focus, for a time, on the means —an open dialogue with her neighbor—rather than the end.

The ideal Gandhian way of thinking about the matter, however, is to do away with the distinction between means and ends altogether. Gandhi saw the relationship between these two not in the mechanical cause-and-effect way that we usually do; instead, he saw the relationship as hydraulic, with one flowing naturally from the other. He also employed a biological metaphor, describing the connection between the means and the ends as that between a seed and the tree that emerges naturally from it.

If Gandhi was right and the means and the ends are intertwined inextricably, then our fighting can become disarmingly unconventional. We can use a temporary goal as a means of fighting and then abandon it at the moment when it is no longer relevant to the fight.

Or we can fight without a specific goal at the outset, and hope that our way of fighting will allow one to emerge. The point of doing this is not to confuse the opponent, but to demonstrate a pattern of living in which means and ends have no meaning apart from one another. Our way of fighting should itself bear the integrity we would like to achieve in the outcome of the struggle. For as Gandhi found, some struggles never end, and the only peace to be found is the peace one gains from meeting violence in a nonviolent way.

♣ 7
The Power of Noncooperation

The first principle of nonviolent action is that of noncooperation with everything humiliating.[1]

Let us say that during a fight you have tried to do exactly what the Gandhian approach would have you do: use the goal as a means and the means as a goal. But in both of these ventures, and in every other Gandhian move that you would like to make, you are blocked. Your opponent has you checked, either physically or psychologically.

There are times when we seem to be forced to play the game by the other person's rules rather than by Gandhi's. It would be nice if we could always wage fights in the Gandhian way and contend with one another on the level of principles. We would rather engage our opponents in a struggle to find the truth in each side's positions than be defensive and protective and wary of devious assaults. But this is not always possible.

Perhaps it is least possible at the very outset of a fight. It is then that powerful opponents seem to have the greatest leverage. Their privileged positions allow them to stifle our grand plan to wage a Gandhian fight.

If the unpleasant Mr. C, for instance, happens to be Ms. A's boss or her landlord or the chair of the city housing board to which boundary disputes are referred, Ms. A is in a tight position. He appears to possess the luxury of being able to refuse to fight and being able to intimidate her into abandoning the fight as well. If Mr. C is her landlord and not only builds the fence, but lets her know that he is adding half of the expense of building it onto her rent, what is she to do? Her dilemma is whether she should play the game according to his rules, rules she regards as unjust.

Gandhi's political strategies were often thwarted by just such powerful opponents. His first experiments with *satyagraha* as a technique were undertaken in South Africa, and were conducted in a situation in which the opponent seemed to define all the rules of the game—unjust rules at that. And there were many times when his options seemed as severely limited as Ms. A's.

He discovered that as a person of color he was not allowed to ride in the first class compartments of trains. If he were to ride at all, he would have to do so third class. To Gandhi this would have been tantamount to lending his tacit support to a practice he regarded as shameful and worse. When Gandhi boarded the train, he did not have the luxury of discussing with the authorities the principles at issue, or presenting an alternative resolution to the difficulty. Rather, he was faced with having to decide whether to go along with their system of racial segregation. Gandhi decided, and he refused to have anything to do with the arrangement. He sat where he pleased, first class, and was promptly bounced from the train.

This may not seem much like *satyagraha*, but in fact it is often its first step: "noncooperation with everything humiliating," as Gandhi put it.[2] Such an act of defiance may eventually lead to a *satyagraha* solution if it allows the fighters to sever ties with an unjust and turbulent past and make way for a more fair and harmonious future.

Noncooperation was not invented by Gandhi. The practice of *hartal,* which is much like the tactic of going on strike, is a familiar method of protest in India, and in the West various forms of passive resistance have proven effective in making an opponent more open to resolving a conflict. Hungarians in the mid-nineteenth century refused to pay taxes to the Austrian emperor Franz Josef, and in so doing succeeded in being allowed to create their own constitution. The Boston Tea Party in the century preceding that was a similar instance of resistance to unjustly applied taxes, and in this century forms of noncooperation were used by Jews, Danes, Norwegians, and many others against the invading Nazis. In even more recent years, Americans have refused to sit in the backs of buses, burned their draft cards, and withheld taxes as a symbolic protest against military spending. For many modern activists passive resistance seems to have become the political tactic of preference.

The most familiar form of noncooperation in the modern West is not political, however, but economic: the labor strike. Demands for wages, better working conditions, and shorter hours are frequently on the strikers' lists. By walking out on their jobs, laborers are often able to cripple production and force factory managers to come to the bargaining table.

From a Gandhian point of view, though, strikes have their dangers. The strikers' demands may seem just, but the way in which the strike is waged can render it coercive and therefore incompatible with a Gandhian approach. To determine whether coercion is really at issue, one must look at the facts of each case to see whether the strike took place in the context of reconciliation between workers and managers, and whether the workers allowed their opponents an equal voice in negotiating the outcome. If that framework is absent, then a strike is a form of coercion and would be wrong in Gandhian terms.

So Gandhi would not approve of all campaigns of noncooperation, even those that may appear benign. The justice of the demands is no guarantee that a labor strike, a campaign of passive resistance, or any other form of noncooperation ought to be considered moral. The key is whether the action is conducted as a part of *satyagraha,* There are times when it is appropriate to refuse to cooperate, and times when it is not.

Gandhi asserted that the difference between his form of noncooperation and the passive resistance that others had sometimes employed was as great as the difference between "the North Pole and the South." According to Gandhi,

> Passive resistance has been conceived as a weapon of the weak and does not exclude the use of physical force or violence for the purpose

of gaining one's end, whereas *satyagraha* has been conceived as a weapon of the strongest and excludes the use of violence in any shape or form.[3]

An unacceptable form of passive resistance, then, is one that is coercive. Gandhian noncooperation, by contrast, is never that, and can rightly be employed only as a means of disengaging both participants from their narrow positions in a fight. If an existing conflict has become so rigidified that participants cannot move toward the Gandhian goal of an alternative order, then noncooperation may be the only way to break the logjam. That move is apt to be disruptive and to catch the opponent off guard, but the disruption should not be used to make the opponent comply unwillingly.

In the case of Ms. A and Mr. C, for example, even if Ms. A feels that she has no options in the fight, she can refuse to go along with anything that seems to her to be patently wrong. She can refuse to pay the portion of the rent that is earmarked for the fence, for instance. And she can resist anything else connected with what she feels is C's misguided and self-serving attempt to resolve the issue in his own favor. She might even slip through the fence and go on planting the garden on his side as well as hers. The point would be to show him what he's missing by sticking so obstinately to his own preconceptions. Her actions may well be regarded as impudent by Mr. C, however, and she may well risk verbal abuse or arrest or some other form of retaliation from him. But there is also the possibility that Mr. C may be shocked enough at her refusal to go along with his commands that he will enter into a new phase of dialogue. Then true *satyagraha* might finally commence.

It may seem that even this degree of noncooperation involves an element of force. And so it does: noncooperation is a kind of forcefulness. But as we have seen, the Gandhian fighter makes a great distinction between force that coerces and force that encourages.

In the Gandhian view, the latter is the only acceptable kind of force. Gandhi assumed that most people, given the chance and a little encouragement, would want to do the right thing. He placed great faith in human nature, and felt that free choice was the prerequisite to a moral resolution. People had to have "the liberty to do evil," Gandhi reasoned, "before they have the ability to do good."[4]

Noncoercive force allows an opponent to make a free choice, even though it presents the truthful option in a forceful way. Coercive force, on the other hand, permits no options other than that intended by the one who forces. For that reason, coercive force is a form of violence. It lowers the opponent's dignity to the level of a caged animal. Even though it may be called nonviolent passive resistance and there may be no physical force involved, if the force is coercive it bears the mark of violence all the same. In Gandhi's lexicon, only an approach that is genuinely noncoercive can be called nonviolent.

It may appear that only a thin line separates these two sorts of force, but to Gandhians that hairsbreadth makes all the difference. Those who try to follow the Gandhian rules are well aware that the achievements of many of their fights, including those waged by Gandhi himself, have been discounted as coercion masquerading as nonviolence. Though they deny these accusations, the criticism has made Gandhians especially sensitive to the distinction between nonviolent force and coercion. Much energy and soulsearching have been spent deliberating over the difference, even—in fact, especially —in the midst of a battle.

There is a good reason why noncooperation may look like coercion even when it is not: the refusal to submit to a command can be quite empowering. The weak and defenseless Ms. A may suddenly appear strong if she refuses to cooperate with the powerful Mr. C. She becomes a threat to his orderly world, and that ability to disrupt and alter his life gives her a degree of power that she previously did not have.

She is in an especially good position to wield the weapon of unpredictability. She has the ability to incapacitate a system of authority simply by refusing to go along with it at some point that only she has the power to determine. This power has been described as "moral jiu jitsu,"[5] since the person who uses it can throw an oppo-

nent off balance by refusing to respond in kind to a blow or a taunt
or an unjust rule.

Such actions often require great courage, for the response to
them is apt to be fury, even violence. The opponents may have
thought they were dealing with someone of little consequence, and
now find that weakling challenging their authority, threatening to
disrupt their orderly world. When Martin Luther King, Jr., and his
fellow fighters for civil rights refused to cooperate with racially dis-
criminatory laws and practices, the response from many in authority
was vitriolic. And in some tragic cases, blood was shed and lives
were lost.

The response of upper caste people in India to the protests of
Untouchables has frequently been the same. The tactic of noncooperation has traditionally been the major weapon—often the only
weapon—that Untouchables have been able to employ. For that
reason, Gandhian protests on behalf of and by Untouchables have
often employed the technique of noncooperation. One such protest,
in the town of Kotgarh in the Himalayan foothills in 1921, was
waged against the practice of forcing Untouchables to do free labor.
With the assistance of Gandhian organizers, the Untouchables
banded together and refused to do any labor until they were paid.
Ultimately the campaign was successful, but not without a great deal
of hostility and even violence from the opposition.

The fears expressed by those in power when an army of opponents ceases to cooperate with them are genuine and warranted.
After all, the ability to disrupt is a potent force, for structures of
authority are fragile things built on thin threads of trust between
those who lead and those who assent to their leadership. Noncooperation threatens to sever those ties and bring the whole construct
down. In the jargon of the social sciences this is called delegitimiza-
tion, the refusal to credit those in authority with the legitimacy that
gives their position its power. Hence even a single dissenter in an
army can be the cause of enormous concern because rebellion can
quickly spread throughout the ranks. When a whole group of
people refuse to obey the rules, the response from those in power
may be sheer panic.

Gandhi cautioned his fighters to be aware of the power of non-cooperation and not to use that power capriciously. In a mass movement of noncooperation against the Rowlatt Bills in 1919, for instance, he felt that the force of noncooperation had gone awry, and halted the movement. He did not want his followers to use the force of noncooperation to cause a disruption that would in any way harm the opponent or coercively force the opponent's hand. Instead, the strength that is gained through noncooperation is supposed to be like that of the weapons worn by armed guards: by being displayed, they never need to be discharged.

Yet it was very important to Gandhi that his nonviolent fighters be regarded as powerful. He abhorred the idea that *satyagraha* could be seen as a "cover for cowardice."[6] He wanted it to be understood as something possible "only for the strong."[7] By strength, he meant the strength that comes through an indomitable will and a fearless resolve. Yet he would not deny that his ability to disrupt also provided a strong leverage against the powerful, and that his notion of strength involved an ability to control and even to coerce. One must have "the power to punish," Gandhi once said, before one can have "the power to pity and forgive."[8]

Noncooperation, then, is a potent weapon in the armory of Gandhian fighters. It gives them a sudden strength where they may have had little before, and it allows them to disengage themselves from an untruthful situation. For both these reasons, an act of noncooperation may signal that an impasse in a fight has been overcome, and that *satyagraha* has begun.

8
Fighting a Very Big Fight

Let me not be misunderstood. Strength does not come from physical capacity. It comes from an indomitable will.[1]

So far we have been considering fights waged on a fairly modest scale. A quarrel over property rights, a clash between coworkers —these are the sorts of disagreements that you and I encounter often in our daily lives. They are also the kind that are usually resolved fairly easily through a nonviolent, compromising approach.

Gandhi himself used this approach in interpersonal situations such as these, and he credited his wife with a rather special skill in what he described as "domestic satyagraha"[2]—family fights. But Gandhi is best known for the large political campaigns that he waged in labor disputes and in the cause of India's movement for independence from British rule. These involved thousands, even tens of thousands of people.

What if we were to be involved in a struggle of such epic proportions—would we fight these large campaigns any differently than the small, interpersonal ones? Did Gandhi?

The answer is essentially no. The same basic rules apply no matter how large the issue or how strong the opponent: satyagraha in all cases requires a search for a truthful and harmonious alternative to conflict, and in all cases one must keep a tight grip on a tentative solution (if a tentative solution is appropriate at this point) as one proceeds to try to win the opponent over to the endeavor of finding the right outcome.

The very scale of the conflict, however, can lead to significant alterations in the way that search for a solution and that attempt to convert the opponent are waged. The struggle of the Solidarity Union against the Polish government, for instance, is not a simple encounter between Lech Walesa and a few government officials. The union engages hundreds of thousands of workers acting in concert, and not one government but a whole network of governments is involved. Crucial to the strength of the Polish labor movement is its ability to act as a single unified entity. Since its number is large, and its struggle protracted, Solidarity needs an effective means of communication, and needs discipline of a "special rigid sort," as Gandhi put it.[3] At a minimum, the Polish workers need to be trained in joint action and need to agree on a method of collective decision-making if they are to act in accord and not send their opponent mixed signals about their intentions.

So far I have said nothing that is specifically Gandhian. These guidelines for organizing a large campaign could apply to any kind of movement for resistance, whether it is composed of nonviolent *satyagrahis,* coercive strikers or armed soldiers. How is the Gandhian cadre different in organization from the others?

The answer may surprise you: very little. The Gandhians' method of making decisions sets them apart—they will prefer a form of *satyagraha,* a method of consensus—but their forces are apt to be just as tightly organized as any other. In fact, there is an even greater need for coordination and communication in a Gandhian campaign than in a coercive or violent campaign. Since the opponent usually expects such a large group to be militant, and even brutal, the Gandhian side must execute some rather skillful maneuvers to demonstrate that it is different. And that requires immaculate organization. Gandhians depend on their ability to build delicate ties of trust with their opponents, and that trust is easily shattered if a Gandhian group sends contradictory signals, or if some of its number succumb to the temptation of using violent means.

During the independence struggle in India when a massive demonstration of civil disobedience against British authorities turned ugly and some of the demonstrators resorted to violence—a few even to murderous assaults—Gandhi called it a "Himalayan miscalculation" on his part to assume that they were all prepared for *satyagraha*. In fact, he discovered that many had "never learnt the art,"[4] and he immediately canceled the event.

Gandhi sometimes compared a *satyagraha* struggle with war, and Gandhian fighters with soldiers: "In satyagraha and military warfare the position of the soldier is very nearly the same," he claimed, pointing out that a *satyagrahi*, like a soldier, "knows no rest, no certainty of movements." Both "face heavy odds and even death," and both are bound "to be under discipline and obey the general's command."[5] He insisted that nonviolent strategies had to be planned with as much discipline and care as if they were battle maneuvers.

The difficulty, of course, is that many conflicts *are* wars. An opponent may be quite willing to fight violently, even murderously, regardless of the Gandhian side's commitment to nonviolence. So a Gandhian fighter must be trained to persist in nonviolent techniques even when violence threatens. This means that Gandhians must be willing, if necessary, to take the brunt of the suffering in the battles they wage, even if this means enduring physical pain. When the followers of Martin Luther King, Jr., were set upon by guard dogs and threatened with clubs, Gandhi would have been pleased that they persevered, and he would even have admired the courage of many to persevere even in the face of life-threatening opposition. Gandhi advised his followers "not only not to fear death, but to face it and welcome it when it comes in the performance of duty."[6]

The mention of pain may make you wonder if the sufferings that Gandhi and his followers have endured are not themselves a form of violence—violence to the self. Gandhi did not see the matter this way, however; he said that suffering incurred in a Gandhian struggle was not self-inflicted, but rather accepted, and "with the purest of motives." Even though Gandhians may allow themselves to suffer, to do so is "an expression of nonviolence."[7] Gandhi reasoned that in such cases the spirit of violence is already abroad, not manufactured by the nonviolent warrior. Such a person merely serves to shoulder the burden of what is already there.

Gandhi invoked a traditional Hindu term for ascetic discipline and self-abnegation to characterize suffering willingly endured: he called it *tapasya*. Such ascetic practices carry a certain religious sanction in India, but even so there is a great deal of discussion in Gandhian circles as to whether and when acceptance of suffering can be allowed.

We will return to this difficult issue later, but for right now suffice it to say that Gandhi felt he could discern the difference between *tapasya* and violence. In fact he insisted that a certain amount of self-denial is absolutely necessary in a Gandhian struggle. If the opponent is powerful, Gandhi thought, the fighter must be able to subjugate all personal interests in the battle—even, if necessary, the basic human interest in personal safety. The point of doing so is to demonstrate the collective power of the movement of which the fighter is a part, and the strength of its resolve.

Mounting a large nonviolent campaign is, as William James said, "the moral equivalent to war."[8] And it does indeed take enormous strength. Gandhi claimed that he had that power, but that his strength was based on the size and resolve of his movement, not on coercive might. A strength based on size and resolve requires mobilization and discipline. One of the first steps in a large Gandhian campaign, therefore, is the recruiting and training necessary to create such an organization.

How large an organization needs to be created depends largely on the nature of the struggle and the size of the opponent. If the opponent is powerful and the principle at issue is of fundamental importance, then a multitude may be required. In the struggle with the British, Gandhi had to mobilize much of the country. If his side were to have been as "weak in numbers as the British," Gandhi felt it might well have been tempted to resort to the same method the British used, that is, "terrorism and deception."[9]

Gandhian fighters sometimes take on larger issues and greater opponents than they are able to combat; this is one of their most frequent failings. Compared with the hundreds of thousands Gandhi rallied in his campaigns against the British, a small number of pro-

testers picketing a federal building in an American city may seem
patently impotent. If their aim is to appeal to the communications
media in an attempt to educate the wider public, however, a small
group may be enough. Even so, eventually more Gandhian troops
will be required.

In some situations small numbers can be compensated for by
intense resolve. When a handful of people chain themselves to the
doors of a federal building, it is highly likely they will be noticed.
(The message they project must be clear, however, or the point they
are making will be lost.) A certain strength can be gained through
this sort of symbolic *satyagraha*, particularly if members of a group
are willing to undertake actions that show the depth of their commitment. When a small group of protestors against the Vietnam war
poured blood on Pentagon records, for instance, it made a powerful
statement. Gandhi claimed that "the force of numbers is not always
necessary" in fighting for a just cause,[10] and that there are moments
when the severity of an issue requires a dramatic if lonely demonstration of moral courage to draw public attention to its importance.

Gandhi argued that in most cases, however, a strategy for waging
satyagraha needs to be tailored in proportion to the circumstances
of the conflict. But whatever the size of the campaign, the Gandhian
rules do not change. The tactics chosen have to be consistent with
the goal of bringing about a harmonious resolution between the
opposing forces.

The tactics most frequently applied by Gandhi himself in large
campaigns against the British included mass demonstrations, strikes,
and acts of civil disobedience. Demonstrations had the multiple effects of mobilizing the supporters, demonstrating the strength of the
movement, and dramatically presenting the Gandhian position on
the issue. The other tactics were efforts to accomplish the same
results while at the same time refusing to cooperate with a system or
set of laws Gandhi and his followers regarded as unjust.

Gandhi's use of these tactics is presented and analyzed in a sys-
tematic fashion by Joan Bondurant in *Conquest of Violence*.[11] She
identifies several steps in a typical *satyagraha* campaign, which may
be summarized as follows.

The campaign begins with attempts to negotiate and discuss the issue. If these fail, a larger group is mobilized and trained for nonviolent action. The first such action is a public demonstration of the Gandhians' grievances, followed by a presentation to the opponent of the resolution to the conflict as envisioned in Gandhian terms.

If this resolution is not accepted, and if the opponent fails to express interest in negotiating some other settlement, then the Gandhians begin to withdraw from the opponent's way of doing things. This may involve boycotts, strikes, other forms of noncooperation, and instances of civil disobedience.

The Gandhians hope that these measures will encourage the opponent to reconsider any refusal to discuss the issue—if that has been the case—and will help to forge a resolution that is agreeable to both sides. But if it does not, the Gandhians may create a parallel entity to replace the organizations erected by the opponent: a parallel government, for example, or an alternative structure of factory management. If this entity is accepted as legitimate by those it governs or manages, an effort to scrap the old order can be mounted.

It is unlikely that the old order will gracefully fade away. Nonetheless, the attempt to create parallel structures may prove to be the factor that provokes the leaders of the old regime to consider negotiation even after earlier attempts have failed.

At least this is what the Gandhian fighters hope will happen. If, however, this strategy too is frustrated, then the measures are escalated. At each point it is hoped that the other side will agree to join in the discussion to seek a harmonious resolution. But if it does not, an even more assertive form of confrontation and engagement will be pursued.

The ultimate weapon of Gandhian fighters is to take a stand of absolute commitment to a principle, and be so willing to internalize the violence of the conflict that one is ready to perish for one's position. Such a tactic was pursued by Gandhi on several occasions, in the form of fasts unto death.

This is a dangerous tactic, for it has the potential of being highly coercive as well as violent toward oneself, and Gandhi applied it only as a last resort. But he denied that his use of it was harmful, speaking of fasting instead as an "influence of love."[12] Whether Gandhi's own logic actually legitimates the use of fasts as a tactic of political manipulation is a matter of some dispute. Gandhi himself admitted that the "dividing line between a selfish and unselfish" use of fasting was "often very thin."[13] But however one may feel about this issue, one must be impressed with Gandhi's determination and the strength that comes only with such extreme forms of commitment and resolve.

The end of any Gandhian fight arrives only when both sides agree on the same principle. In a large campaign, this means that all members of both sides must come to that agreement. And since thousands of persons may be involved, the ultimate completion of a large *satyagraha* campaign may involve a program of communication and education among the rank-and-file that must continue long after the leaders have been won over.

Satyagraha on an extremely large scale will require nothing less than a "nonviolent revolution,"[14] the recreation of whatever societies are involved in the conflict. This was precisely Gandhi's vision for India and Britain. He was willing to consider his struggle for India's independence complete only when the two countries were free from their dependence on one another and internally strong as well.

Steps in Waging a Large Campaign

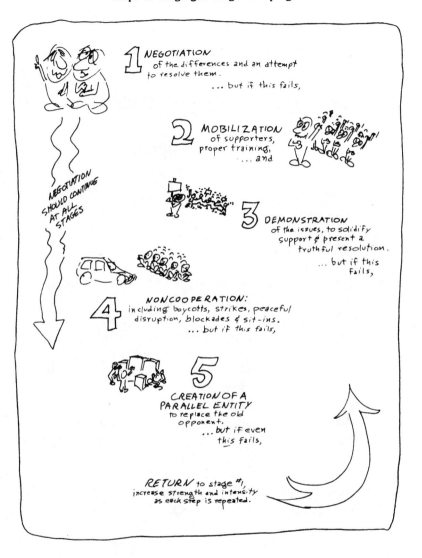

1 NEGOTIATION of the differences and an attempt to resolve them.
... but if this fails,

2 MOBILIZATION of supporters, proper training, ... and

3 DEMONSTRATION of the issues, to solidify support & present a truthful resolution.
... but if this fails,

NEGOTIATION SHOULD CONTINUE AT ALL STAGES

4 NONCOOPERATION: including boycotts, strikes, peaceful disruption, blockades & sit-ins.
... but if this fails,

5 CREATION OF A PARALLEL ENTITY to replace the old opponent.
... but if even this fails,

RETURN to stage #1, increase strength and intensity as each step is repeated.

How Do You Know
When You've Won?

A nonviolent revolution is not a seizure of power. It is a transformation of relationships, ending in a peaceful transfer.[1]

In an ordinary fight, it is fairly clear when the battle is over. If you have won, you've won. If you have lost, you go off sulking.

But Gandhian fights are not ordinary fights. Nobody wins until everybody wins, and that could take a long time. In the meantime there are intermediate victories, of a sort. But even these may look peculiar from a non-Gandhian perspective.

In a textile mill labor dispute in which Gandhi was involved, the mill owners eventually conceded to a higher wage rate, and their striking laborers agreed to it even though it was not as high as many of them had desired. The laborers accepted the settlement because Gandhi had determined it to be fair, but many of them did so grudgingly, regarding this compromise as something near failure.

But Gandhi did not. For him the heart of the matter was not the money. He claimed it was the principles he cared about, and labor-owner relations. What pleased Gandhi was to see the laborers band together in a community of strength, and to see the mill owners, men whom he admired for their "resolute will and transparent sincerity," apparently bent on restoring a good working relationship with the laborers at the termination of the strike. Out of the strike came a permanent organization, a labor union with an "extensive program of welfare benefits" for its members.[2]

To Gandhi's mind, these actions and attitudes of solidarity and good will constituted the true solution, and he claimed that the strike

was over only when the mill owners and the workers were converted to this solution out of principle. It was not enough that either side
should give in to it passively or accept it out of necessity. Although
some have claimed that Gandhi initially forced the hand of the owners through a coercive use of fasting, Gandhi felt that eventually
they came to accept the principles willingly.

From a Gandhian point of view, the struggle was not resolved for
some time after the agreement was reached. Only later could the
real change in labor-owner relations—or the lack of it—be seen.
No true Gandhian resolution could be proclaimed until both sides
had acted on the principle to which they had agreed, and entered
into a relationship of good will.

Winning, in the Gandhian sense, requires a "transformation of
relationships."[3] It is never simply a matter of conquest.

Some of the most difficult victories to "win," from a Gandhian
point of view, are cases of conflict in which the truth is consistently
on one side rather than the other. The untruthful side has to make
some admission of the bankruptcy of its stand, and the truthful side
has to be generous enough to make room for the other in the new
resolution, to "guarantee the freedom" of the opponent.[4] Pride may
hinder both sides.

In our hypothetical case involving the quarreling neighbors, for
instance, it might have been easy for Ms. A to convince everyone
else that she was right. Eventually she might have convinced Mr. B
or even the curmudgeonly Mr. C. But even if he agreed that her
idea of having a jointly tended garden was absolutely right and that
his idea of wanting the land selfishly for himself was a dreadful
mistake, Ms. A might still have problems. The difficulty then would
be in finding a way of honoring Mr. C, "guaranteeing his freedom,"
as Gandhi put it, and keeping him from feeling like conquered prey.

The fight is not over—the truthful way does not fully win out—
until Mr. C emerges from the conflict with his dignity intact. The
Gandhian logic about honoring life is the rule applicable here. Even
if Mr. C is wrong about everything else, he is heir to one immutable
truth. He is due the respect owed to every person, "the right of free
opinion and free action."[5] And this has to be taken into account

before it can finally be said that the fight has been won, the conflict resolved.

From the Gandhian point of view, therefore, what looks like a full victory may be only the successful conclusion of a skirmish. And by the same token what looks like defeat may sometimes be a victorious resolution.

For example, one side may succeed in persuading the other that contrary to first appearances it was right all along. Mr. B, or even his dour replacement, Mr. C, may be able to argue his position in a less self-serving and more compelling way than he did at first. He may convince Ms. A that good fences do indeed make for good neighbors, and that a ten foot high barricade beside the rhododendrons will set their relationship right. If Ms. A sees the wisdom of that, and honestly feels that his solution will be best for both of them, she may concede. Then truth will win out, even if it is not the truth that she had earlier envisaged.

In other instances, unexpected new solutions might appear just when both sides think that the fight is over. A broader perspective on the conflict is one factor that could alter the way the solution is posed. If Ms. A engages some of the other neighbors in her conflict with Mr. C, for instance, they might persuade her that her goal of a garden held jointly between her and Mr. C is too narrow a solution. They might prefer a more inclusive outcome, one based on the principle that any unused land in the area should serve as common space for the whole community. A compost pit or a neighborhood garden might, from their point of view, do just fine.

Ms. A might agree. And if she does become convinced of the truthfulness of their proposal, she will have to change her goal.

Other considerations too might cause her to change her tactics. She might, on reflection, feel that her use of aggressive tactics (such as mounting a massive letter-writing campaign against him) was a miscalculation as Himalayan as Gandhi's, and on account of the same principle: when tactics become destructive rather than affirming, they must be abandoned. In some instances tactics are faulty not because they lead directly to violence, but because they are destructive in an indirect sense. They may intimidate the opponent, "give rise to hatred,"[6] as Gandhi put it, and close off lines of communication rather than opening them.

A Gandhian fight requires one to experiment with tactics and goals; both may be changed. On some occasions one may even need to redefine one's opponent. If Ms. A and Mr. C were to come to the conclusion that their real difficulty is not with each other but with the nature of property laws, they might join forces in a fight to have these laws changed. The fight would be continued in a different arena; the sides themselves would have been realigned.

The one thing that stays constant in a Gandhian fight is the commitment to finding a harmonious resolution: "insistence on truth."[7] Yet there are times when that commitment and that insistence do not seem to lead to any final truth or resolution at all. The opponent never changes or gives in. The fighting never ends. Ms. A and Mr. C could grow old growling at each other over that little bit of unhappy, unused land.

Gandhi himself never advocated abandoning a fight, but he did on occasion accept a lesser solution than he had initially proposed. He would terminate a struggle when the energy expended in waging it outweighed the benefits to be gained from a total victory, an ideal resolution. Pyrrhic victories, in Gandhian thought, are no victories at all.

In other fights he persisted tenaciously. In a 1924 campaign for the rights of Untouchables to use a road leading to an upper caste temple in the town of Vykom in South India, Gandhi directed the protestors to take turns keeping a prayer vigil in front of the police cordon that had been erected to prevent their passage. They continued to stand, even as days and weeks and months passed. During the rainy season the road was flooded, and the protestors kept their vigil standing in water up to their shoulders as the police patrolled the barricade in small boats. Finally, after a year and four months, when it seemed that the vigil would never end, the opposition relented and the policy was changed.

In still other fights, Gandhi acquiesced after a long stalemate, even though it seemed to some that the fight was still worth waging. Gandhi did not agree. He felt that the impasse signaled that somehow his strategy was wrong. In such cases he would sometimes to go back to the very beginning steps of *satyagraha* and examine his own position, not only to analyze the efficacy of the tactics, but to see whether his pride had prohibited an accurate assessment of the truthful and untruthful elements in his position. When he succeeded in finding the flaws, he would attempt to "mend his error" and "start the movement again."[8]

There is still a final possibility to be faced: some fights may go on forever.

Despite the victories achieved in the struggle for civil rights in the United States, the movement inaugurated by Martin Luther King, Jr., has yet to end. The struggle is still being waged by leaders who from time to time attempt to revive the spirit that King so eloquently represented. And despite the cessation of hostilities in Vietnam, many of the activists from the antiwar movement continue to fight against what they regard as the real culprit: America's posture of militarism and its drive toward global dominance. So even though others cheered the ending of the Vietnam war and then forgot it, for these persistent activists the fight goes on.

As dismal as the idea of endless fighting may seem, one might argue that at the deepest level the Gandhian wishes for nothing less. In the Gandhian sense, a fight exists wherever there is a state of irresolution and disharmony: untruth. According to the Gandhian ideal the fighter should not rest until the opposite is achieved—truth —and that means never, for there are always wrongs to be righted, always fragments to be made whole.

The endless fighting of the Gandhian is not a quixotic venture, however, for the very act of struggle can be its own reward. Gandhi claimed that a *satyagraha* campaign is always "worthy," because at the very least it leaves those who wage it "stronger and more spirit-ed" than when they started.[9] Such a fight clarifies truth and makes it more accessible, and saves the fighter from doing nothing of substance at all. In the Gandhian view, you begin to win as soon as the fight begins; and you always win something, even if the fighting never ends.

♣ 10
Some Basic Rules

1. **Do not avoid confrontation.**
   Avoidance simply prolongs the underlying conflict between principles. Instead, you should welcome an encounter between positions, and the clarity it brings. (See Chapters 1 and 2.)
2. **Stay open to communication and self-criticism.**
   Each side in a conflict has only a partial view. It needs the critical perspective of the other to sort out truth from untruth. (See Chapter 2.)
3. **Find a resolution and hold fast to it.**
   Once a harmonious alternative becomes apparent, you should seize onto it and base your strategy on it—but be willing to challenge and change it as well. (See Chapter 3.)
4. **Regard your opponent as a potential ally.**
   Do nothing to harm or alienate your opponent. Remember your goal is to join forces to struggle together against untruth. (See Chapters 4 and 5.)
5. **Make your tactics consistent with the goal.**
   Use the goal itself as the weapon for fighting, when possible. When not, use only those actions that are consistent with it. (See Chapter 6.)
6. **Be flexible.**
   Be willing to change tactics, alter proximate goals, revise your notion of who your opponent is, and even reconsider your conception of the truth. (See Chapters 7 and 9.)
7. **Be temperate.**
   Escalate your actions by degrees. The idea is to keep your

opponent from feeling intimidated, so that he or she will be communicative rather than defensive in responding to you. (See Chapter 8.)

8. **Be proportionate.**

Determine which issues are trivial and which deserve your time and energy. The basis for judgment is the degree to which life and the quality of life are abused. Mount a campaign with a strength equal to that of the opponent, and appropriate to the issue. (See Chapters 3, 4, and 8.)

9. **Be disciplined.**

Especially when a large number is involved in a collective effort, make certain that your side is committed to a nonviolent approach and that your position is coherent. Consistency is one of your strengths. (See Chapter 8.)

10. **Know when to quit.**

A deadlocked campaign, or one with negative results, may require that you revise your tactics and perhaps even change your proximate goals. A concession to your side without an agreement on principle is not victory. In a Gandhian fight, you can claim to have won only if your opponent can say the same. (See Chapter 9.)

SECTION II:
CASE STUDIES

❧ Looking at Cases

How do the Gandhian ideas hold up in actual situations? With this question in mind, we turn to several, quite varied cases of conflict—a domestic squabble, a labor-management dispute, a personal decision, a social crusade, and a situation of massive political oppression.

These cases were chosen because they represent a wide range of conflict situations. I have deliberately avoided including Gandhi's own encounters, in part because these have been thoroughly examined already by Joan Bondurant and other scholars, and in part because I wanted to see if the Gandhian approach could apply to a range of cases that you and I might actually confront.

Most of the participants in the struggles that follow have never heard of the Gandhian approach. But this makes no difference for our purposes, since we are going to use *satyagraha* as a yardstick to gauge any attempt to resolve a conflict. Those who consciously try to follow Gandhi's ideals may fare no better than those for whom the nonviolent path comes quite naturally.

Each of the cases that follow is based on a real situation, and will be described as it was actually waged and resolved. We will see that certain sorts of conflicts lend themselves more easily to *satyagraha* than others, but that any fight can be seen as embodying some element of the Gandhian struggle for truth. The question is how much, how well the game is played according to Gandhian rules.

The Gandhian game of conflict resolution begins with an identification of the opponents and the central issue over which they are struggling. The descriptions of the cases will begin the same way, even though in fact some fights founder precisely because those who participate in the struggle leave the issues and the adversaries ill defined.

We will also look behind the positions of the opponents, as a Gandhian might, and try to identify the principles that are at stake—the real conflicts behind the superficial ones. And the goal of the game—the discovery of an alternative to the conflict that would reconcile these principles—will be identified at the outset of the case description, even though in the actual conflicts such a goal might not have emerged until well into the fight.

A struggle begins, from a Gandhian point of view, at the first indication that a conflict exists. These analyses trace the development of each struggle from this point to its attempted resolution. Along the way any efforts to deal with the conflict in a Gandhian manner will be flagged: attempts to articulate the truthful principles at issue, formulate an alternative to the conflict, or wage a campaign for its acceptance.

♣ Case #1:
A Family Feud

Central Issue: Scheduling the evening meal

Opponents: *Suzanne v. Mike*

Principles at Stake: Individual freedom and integrity; the need for order and predictability; maturity in their roles and relationships

Attempted resolution: Suzanne and Mike build flexibility into the schedule and share responsibility for maintaining it.

Sequence of Events:

STAGE 1: The emergence of the conflict. During the three years that Suzanne and Mike have been together, Mike has consistently come home late for dinner. Six o'clock is the agreed time, but often as not six comes and goes without a sign of Mike. After several evenings in a row in which the meal has gotten cold, Suzanne decides that she's had enough. She confronts Mike with her anger.

He defends himself by arguing that success in his work depends in part on his camaraderie with his colleagues, and that means occasionally having a drink at the end of the day or joining a coworker at the gym. Spontaneity is the key to the success of these social events, and often there is no way to telephone or to warn Suzanne in advance.

Suzanne, for her part, has graduate studies to attend to. Even if Mike calls to tell her he will be late, a delay in dinner plans can dismantle the whole evening's schedule.

After their initial confrontation, Mike promises to be more considerate. Suzanne apologizes for being so irritable, they make up and make love, and everything is forgotten. That is, until the same thing happens again the next week.

This time Suzanne is not so forgiving. She decides not to hide the conflict but let it surface, to grapple with it in what Gandhi called "domestic *satyagraha.*"[1]

STAGE 2: The search for truth. Suzanne, in an only partially successful attempt to control her feelings, explains that she really has had enough of this unpredictability, and begins to deliver the casserole to the sink. Mike is apologetic but insistent on his right to be independent. Suzanne defends her own rights, especially the right to have some sense of certainty about her schedule.

Suzanne searches for a compromise—she will let him be late once a week—but this suggestion seems only to provoke Mike. She is trying to tie him down, he complains, claiming that in addition to his need to socialize with his colleagues, he needs to express his own identity.

They also consider eating separately, but neither of them is in favor of this solution. Their evening meals have been times when they have felt close to one another, and eating apart would symbolize a distance in their relationship that neither is willing to acknowledge.

They go to bed without making up, and sleep comes fitfully for both. In the middle of the night, as the matter tumbles through her mind, Suzanne comes to the realization that she is being treated like a short order cook, and that she should not be expected to prepare meals for Mike if he doesn't have the courtesy to show up on time. She wakes him to announce her decision, more or less in those terms.

STAGE 3: The campaign for acceptance begins. Mike is no more persuaded of the rectitude of her position now than before, and Suzanne decides that she has to take some sort of action.

Her primary tactic is passive resistance. That is, on those evenings when Mike doesn't show up on time, Suzanne eats by herself and consigns the rest to Vivaldi, their pet spaniel. When Mike returns and the dinner has disappeared, he feels a bit betrayed, and claims that she is trying to pressure him in order to get her own way.

Mike offers his own solution to the dilemma. On nights when he stays out late, he says, he will either eat out or cook for himself. This suggestion leaves Suzanne even more displeased than before. From her point of view such an arrangement would only serve to facilitate what she sees as the underlying irritant, Mike's unpredictability. Suzanne dismisses Mike's suggestion, and dismisses him from their bed that night as well. He sleeps with Vivaldi on the couch, but neither Mike nor Suzanne sleeps very well.

STAGE 3a: The campaign is reconsidered. At breakfast, the silence is broken by a comment from Mike that Suzanne broods over throughout the day. He says that she is out to control him, even emasculate him. Suzanne does not pursue the matter, but the weightiness of the remark surprises her, and she begins to suspect that their disagreement has gone too far. In thinking about Mike's remark she recalls something he had said on the first day of their argument, something that suggested he felt his identity was under threat.

She tries to reconstruct the situation as Mike might see it. She wonders if making him show up punctually every night makes him feel like a child, like a tethered little boy. And she wonders if dismissing him from their bed the night before made him feel even more infantile since he was denied the expression of his adult sexuality.

But there is the other side to consider as well. Her own adult independence requires a regular schedule. She can't spend the evenings waiting for him to come home. She realizes the irony in their dilemma: they each want the independence that maturity offers, but all of their previous solutions seemed to grant it only to one of them, withholding it from the other.

Suzanne begins to work on formulating a new resolution. Central to it is the idea that Mike should be able to come home late when he wishes, and that she should be able to depend on some regularity in their schedule. She develops a plan and presents it to Mike. She suggests that they switch their evening meal from the usual six o'clock time to nine. Hors d'oeuvres will always be available in the refrigerator at six o'clock for whoever is there to eat them. As for the nine o'clock repast, it will be an elegant affair, and afterward, she hints, even more delicious things will follow.

STAGE 4: The outcome. Initially Mike is skeptical. But Suzanne is enthusiastic about the new resolution, and decides the best way to encourage Mike to join her is to begin to enact it. Every evening the snacks are ready, prepared the night before, and even if Mike is in the mood for dinner at that time he must wait, for often Suzanne will take advantage of the new schedule to tarry at the library.

Eventually Mike becomes used to the idea, but there is still some fine tuning to be done. For one thing, Suzanne finds it wearing that she is still the main cook every night. At the same time Mike is not comfortable forever playing the role of helper as Suzanne tries to concoct yet another splendid entree.

Again a verbal skirmish ensues. Mike tells Suzanne he dislikes being treated like "Mommy's little helper," and Suzanne tells him that she enjoys being Mommy even less. Mike is curiously quiet for a minute, then claims he had not realized that his attitude had helped to cast her in that role, or that she was unhappy about playing it. They end up vowing to find a way that will overcome this deep source of conflict between them, and they make love meaningfully for the first time in weeks.

Their revised solution is to share the responsibility for preparing the food. Suzanne initially finds it difficult to relinquish her dominant role in the kitchen, and she is not always patient as Mike learns to prepare what seems to her to be the most mundane fare. But in time she finds it a small price to pay for an increased freedom, a liberation from old schedules and from old constricting roles.

Comments:

In this case, what begins as a simple, even trivial squabble over the household schedule reveals in time issues more interesting and more fundamental to the couple's relationship. It also uncovers feelings of uncertainty about their personal identities. The fight itself opens up these levels of insight, and clears the path towards an apparently workable resolution.

But is the fight waged in a Gandhian way?

Not initially. The male partner in this domestic drama does little to initiate any movement toward reconciliation other than to articulate his own feelings. Suzanne's opening position is not much better. With righteous indignation, she sees the situation largely from her own point of view.

Both of their attempts at compromise are rejected by the other—indeed they seem to fan the flames of discord. Suzanne's offer to let Mike be late one night a week and Mike's offer to eat by himself are both taken by the other as affronts rather than serious attempts to heal the rift.

Suzanne's attempt to use noncooperation seems to bring mixed results as well. On the one hand her refusal to cook and to sleep with Mike forces the issue into the open. Initially it gives her a form of leverage, which she needs to balance his strong suit, his freedom to come home when he pleases. On the other hand the tactic works almost too well; Mike recoils from what he regards as her coerciveness.

Mike's reaction, however, sets the stage for the critical moment of awareness that comes the following morning. It is good that Suzanne's attempt to manipulate things in her favor fails, for the failure shatters her illusion that her own vision of how things should be is necessarily best for both of them. As a result she begins a search for truth in earnest: she attempts to balance her own view of the situation with what she constructs as his.

In her mind she tallies up the truthful aspects of both of their positions as follows:

Suzanne's Position	*Mike's Position*
1. Dependability in their schedule	1. Flexibility in their schedule
2. Independence	2. Independence
3. Feeling of maturity	3. Feeling of maturity
4. Desire to control	4. Desire to shirk responsibilities

She affirms the first three on each side as legitimate: her need for dependability, his for flexibility, and both of their desires for independence and maturity. She then tries to weave these positive elements into a Gandhian solution. This turns out to be an early evening snack at a flexible time, with a later meal at a fixed time, for which they ultimately agree to share cooking responsibilities.

Like a true Gandhian, Suzanne uses the goal as the very means of achieving it: the solution of having a late elegant meal is itself offered as the inducement to get Mike to agree. He does, and as he becomes increasingly aware of Suzanne's point of view he accepts the principles on which the solution is based. He is not simply manipulated into it. He does so "consciously and voluntarily," as Gandhian rules require.[2] As time passes, both of them seem to be more satisfied with the final resolution than with the positions they were defending at the beginning.

The conflict, therefore, is resolved in a Gandhian way, despite the fact that neither of the participants has any special skill in Gandhian techniques. What made this possible? The answer to this question may help us explain what sorts of attitudes and attributes are conducive to a Gandhian solution.

To begin with, both parties to the conflict had a strong vested interest in achieving a harmonious outcome. They desired, if at all possible, to keep their home life and their relationship as free from tensions as possible. Moreover, they were concerned about the quality of each other's life, and at least one of them was able to empathize with the other's point of view. This much can be said about many couples, close relatives, and intimate friends.

For that reason, however, many family feuds end in one side capitulating to the other or agreeing to an unjust compromise simply for the sake of keeping the peace. This fight also could have been preempted in just that way, if Suzanne had pretended indifference to Mike's irregular schedule, of if Mike had grudgingly capitulated to her attempts to coerce him into complying with her point of view.

What made this fight different from those of many couples was the nature of the participants: they were stubborn. Or as Gandhi put it, they were able to "speak out and stand up for their convictions."[3]

They stood by the integrity of their positions and refused to accept a solution that did not adequately honor them. This led to a stalemate and a frustration with earlier, one-sided tactics. They were forced to look for another option, and this gave them room to consider a Gandhian alternative.

Yet even then they might not have turned to a more creative solution if they hadn't had the wit to do so. Suzanne, especially, possessed the capacity to transcend a single perspective and imagine other ways of seeing her problem. She did this largely on her own, although it took a critical jab from Mike to jar her preconceptions and enable her to see things his way. As a result she was able to envisage a solution quite different from any she had considered before. At that point she proposed it and saw it through.

It may be that three of the elements we see here—the eagerness for a harmonious outcome, the determination of both sides to stand by the truth, and the ability of both to imagine other options—are necessary prerequisites to a Gandhian solution in every situation of conflict. In the case of the feud between Mike and Suzanne, it is hard to imagine how the outcome could have been achieved without these salient factors. And as we will see in other cases, where these three are absent the ultimate resolution is apt to be neither so tidy nor so kind.

♣ Case #2: The Endangered Employees

Central Issue: The effect that an organizational change will have on employees

Opponents: *Employees v. New Owner*

Principles at Stake: Vitality of the organization; the workers' sense of worthiness

Attempted Resolutions: The owner agrees to accommodate some of the workers; workers attempt to restructure the organization to make room for all of them.

Sequence of Events:

STAGE 1: The emergence of the conflict. The Mason Office Furniture Company is an old family business. For many years it has employed the same 20 or so workers, about half of them in the sales outlet and the other half in a small custom-design furniture manufacturing shop attached to the store. When the workers and the business were younger a certain vitality reigned. In recent years the spirit has flagged, but the company has managed to plod on even so, in a desultory way.

A crisis develops when John Mason, Sr., dies and the ownership passes to his widow, Clara, and his son, John, Jr. Young Mason takes over management of the family business, a development the employees regard as ominous. The young Mason spent a profligate youth devoted to rock music and various forms of rebellion, and has only recently turned his energies to the world of finance and office furniture. Now that fate has put him at the helm of the family business, he has determined to steer a more profitable and lively course. Exactly what course this is remains to be seen. One thing is clear, however: Mason will not tolerate what he regards as deadwood in the family store.

A sense of gloom permeates the place. Rumors abound, fueled by reports from the secretaries in the front office, that the new boss is toying with various schemes for reorganizing the company. One of these would eliminate the custom-design section altogether, and with it possibly a few jobs. Rumor also has it that young Mason is dickering with a large discount office furniture chain; it has considered buying the family company if efficiency rises and profits increase.

STAGE 2: The search for an intermediate position. The situation degenerates as the suspicions of the employees grow and the young owner adopts a defensive, distant posture toward them. The employees begin to meet privately to discuss their options. When Mason gets wind of this, his first inclination is to fire them all and be done with it. He realizes, however, that he would have great difficulty running the company with an entirely new crew, and that his mother would be distressed to see the family's faithful workers so summarily dismissed. Moreover, Mason's lawyer informs him that since the employees have banded together with the intent to organize, they may have certain legal rights that would prevent him from firing them as summarily as he would like. Mason concludes that he will have to make some sort of overture to the workers.

Mason regards Chuck Harrison, the foreman of the custom-design furniture shop, as the most valuable and most influential member of the work crew. He calls Harrison to his office. Mason explains that he has plans for some changes that will require restructuring the organization, but he assures Harrison that if dissension among the workers can be stifled, his own job is secure. Even if the custom-design shop were abandoned, Harrison and several of the most able workers would be kept on in sales or other areas of the company.

To Mason's surprise, Harrison does not accept what Mason regards as a generous plan. Instead Harrison hurriedly calls a meeting with the other employees. At the meeting, the workers vent their feelings about Mason and agree that they regard the custom-design shop to be the most interesting aspect of the business, and the one that gives them the greatest personal satisfaction. If there is to be any organizational restructuring, they say, they want to have a hand in planning it. One option they consider is running the custom-design shop as a semi-autonomous branch of the company, and letting Mason do whatever he wants with the rest of the store.

STAGE 3: Initial campaigns for acceptance. Both Mason and the employees now have the task of trying to persuade the other to accept their solutions. Harrison, representing the employees, informs Mason of the workers' feelings and their suggestion for reorganization. Mason continues to hold out the carrot of continued employment for most of the workers. Behind it, however, is the stick of his determination to go ahead with his plans even if it means firing the whole obstinate lot. The two sides are at a stalemate.

The employees feel that their position is handicapped by their lack of power. In one of their meetings their sense of futility reaches a point of despair. They decide to go on strike.

When Mason hears rumors of the impending walkout, he invites Harrison to his home for a drink. He has much on his mind. Mason talks about the good of the company and his own goals in life. He feels that the workers simply want to keep the company in the inefficient past, and are unable to accept the authority of someone younger than they. He avers that he would like to continue to work with them, at least some of them, but they will have to be able to see his point of view as well as their own.

The foreman returns to the workers, troubled over what he regards as at least a measure of truth in Mason's observations. His comrades, however, feel little of this. They are enraged over Mason's intractable stance, and are determined to go on strike as a show of force of their own.

Harrison finds himself in an awkward position. His sympathies lie with his fellow workers, yet he has begun to see Mason's side too. He is sure, in any case, that a direct confrontation would be pointless, and he decides to go for an end run instead: he contacts Mason's mother. Clara Mason is not directly involved in the business affairs of the company, but over the years she has come to know most of the workers personally, and she is deeply touched that the workers have such proud ideas for continuing some of the traditions of the business that her husband worked so hard to establish. In consequence, she agrees to take the matter to her son.

Mrs. Mason's sympathetic response buoys the spirits of the workers: at last they have some hope that the situation can be solved. And for the first time in years, their productivity rises as well.

Clara Mason discusses the matter with her son and conveys to him her feelings that the vision of her husband should be continued and the loyalty of the workers should be rewarded. John, Jr., regards this as a relatively minor consideration, but is impressed with the problems that could arise if the workers were to carry out their threats and mount a strike. To please her and to appease them, Mason comes up with a new compromise. He will delay plans for reorganization and increase the wages of those workers who remain with the company. But to make the company more efficient, there will have to be a ten-percent cut in the work force; two of the employees will have to leave. Mason will leave it up to the workers to decide which two must go.

Stage 3a: Noncooperation. The workers greet this latest proposal with a storm of protest. They hold an emotionally charged meeting in which they decide that they will not take the responsibility for choosing which two of their number is to be fired, nor will they be "bought off," as they put it, with promises of high salaries. They did not request the increase, and they will not be pacified by it. The mood of the meeting is once again to threaten to go on strike.

At this point in the meeting Clara Mason, who has been invited to attend by Chuck Harrison, rises and speaks her mind. She tells the workers that her son has always been a stubborn and unpredictable lad, and she advises that they should keep that in mind. He would interpret the threat of strike as blackmail, she tells them, and would respond with even less flexibility than before.

Harrison agrees with what Mrs. Mason says and offers a more positive approach. He suggests that they look carefully at Mason's proposal and reject only those parts of it that they feel are illegitimate. If they can accept the rest, they should do so. The workers discuss the matter, and decide that at least one aspect of Mason's position is worth taking into account: the need for the company to be more efficient and economically more solvent. They come up with a plan.

The next day the group announces its decision to Mason, and he greets it with a mixture of emotions. The workers tell him they are not going to go on strike, a decision that pleases him. But they reject his offer of an increase in salary, and that he finds puzzling. What makes him even more suspicious, however, is that they make no reference to his request that they choose two employees to be dismissed.

He soon discovers why: they have no intention of carrying out this request. In telling Mason why the workers have decided to adopt this act of noncooperation, Harrison explains that they have committed themselves instead to increasing the productivity of the company by 10 percent, even if it requires a certain amount of sacrifice on their own. They are even willing to work overtime without additional pay. Mason is apprehensive about the rebellious nature of the proposal, but he remembers that one likely alternative to it is a labor strike, and he is curious about whether their plan to cut production costs on their own might actually succeed. He adopts a wait-and-see attitude.

STAGE 4: The outcome. Productivity rises fairly quickly, and it appears that the workers will meet their production goal on time. There are some hitches on the workers' side, however. Several of their members are not enthusiastic about the plan and are unwilling to make extra efforts to increase productivity. The workers hold a meeting to discuss this problem, and agree that they need some sort of formal organization to provide leadership and instill discipline in their ranks.

When they come to the matter of choosing a leader, Chuck Harrison seems the natural choice. Harrison, however, demurs. He feels that although some sort of productivity council is necessary for the efficient functioning of their work group, the leader of such an entity would come perilously close to usurping the traditional role played by the managers of the company. And that might unnecessarily antagonize Mason. In order to minimize this danger, Harrison proposes that Clara Mason be elected chairperson.

He approaches Mrs. Mason with the idea. She is flattered, but feels that if the logic of her selection is to bring about reconciliation in the company, they have not gone far enough in their thinking. She suggests that the only person who can provide the company with both leadership and the hope of harmony is none other than her son. Although Harrison is initially startled at the suggestion of making John Mason, Jr., the chairperson of the productivity council, he becomes captivated by the idea and soon presents it ot the other workers.

At last report, the workers are considering their options and Mason is considering his. There are three, as they see them: 1) They can both hold firm to their positions, Mason challenging the legitimacy of the productivity council, and the workers threatening a strike in retaliation. 2) Mason can join their council and accept their solution to the problem, now that they have created a role into which he could plausibly fit. 3) Mason can sell his share of the company to the workers and strike out on his own. Fortunately, Clara Mason is willing to give the workers the financial backing they will need if her son chooses this option.

At the moment, the workers are inclined to favor Option #2, although there is still some discussion about what role Mason should be invited to play. Mason is leaning toward Option #3, but will also consider Option #2 if the workers are sufficiently supportive of him, and Option #1 if they're not. Harrison hopes for Option #2, a restructuring that would allow Mason and the employees to work together. But even if Option #3 prevails and the workers have to shoulder the responsibility for managing the company alone, he and

Clara Mason and the workers are confident that they can make a go of it, and bring new life to the old store.

Comments:

Options #2 and #3 both fit the Gandhian requirements for a harmonious resolution, even though Option #3 would have Mason sever his ties with the workers and leave each side on its own. A Gandhian solution does not necessarily require both sides to maintain their relationship: an amicable divorce is sometimes called for. In the last years of the British reign in India, for example, Gandhi came to the conclusion that the only honorable role for the British was back in Britain, and that they should "quit India."

If Mason leaves, it may appear that the workers have succeeded in forcing him out, but the facts of the case are more complicated than that. Things have changed substantially from the beginning of the case to the end; in particular, the company has gone a long way toward achieving the economic efficiency on which Mason insisted. So even if he leaves, he will have left his imprint on the organization. And in the process of struggling with him, the workers have also changed; they have formed an organized unit concerned with the welfare of the whole company and not just with their own personal needs.

If Mason stays, he will have to be involved in a new and cooperative relationship with his workers. The two sides will have to work out a plan for sharing responsibility and allocating authority in the productivity council, and this arrangement will have to be negotiated at the outset. The prognosis is good that they will be able to come to some agreement, since Mason has shown a growing sensitivity to the workers' views, and they have shown an increasing awareness of the problems of management. The struggle at the Mason Company has brought the thinking of the two sides closer together.

At the outset of the dispute such a resolution did not seem possible. Both sides were protective of their own points of view and heavy-handed in defending them. Each resorted to threats: Mason mentioned mass firings, and the workers retaliated with talk of a strike.

These threats served some purpose: they indicated how strongly each side felt about the matter. But they also led to a stalemate. The breakthrough came from personal contacts involving Clara Mason, Chuck Harrison, and John Mason, Jr. In the course of these discussions, the two sides were able to increasingly identify and appreciate the elements involved in each position. These are as follows:

Mason's position	*Employees' position*
1. Personal control over the company	1. Collective control
2. Need for efficiency	2. Enjoyment of working hard and well
3. Desire for great output	3. Desire for high quality
4. Boredom with status quo	4. Boredom with status quo
5. Dislike of anything associated with his father	5. Dislike of upstart youths

Not all of these items are positive. The personal dislikes, for instance, have no place in a Gandhian solution. And the lists show a basic difference in style between the two sides. But they also reveal some areas of agreement and places where negotiation would seem fruitful. These areas, in fact, were the starting points for the several proposals for a solution that have evolved between Mason and the workers.

Considering their earlier stalemate, it seems remarkable that Mason and the workers have the glimmer of an agreeable solution. This came about in part because of the reasonableness of the workers in formulating a response to Mason, and in part because of the cogent way in which the workers advanced it. Their power grew as the case progressed, and when they presented their response to Mason, it carried with it great force. For one thing, they had the financial backing of Mrs. Mason and the legal protection of workers' rights. But they had an internal strength that they created through self-discipline and through the willingness to sacrifice a pay increase and after-hours work time for the good of the company. Their act of noncooperation challenged Mason's authority, but it also demonstrated that the workers were committed to improving the company. Perhaps their power could be called a moral strength, or the strength of acting positively. Without it and the other forms of power they had amassed, the workers would not have been able to wage their campaign successfully. Mason could have ignored their protests and fired them all.

The case illustrates Gandhi's point that *satyagraha* must be conducted from a position of strength rather than weakness. For the most part the means of obtaining that strength was compatible with the workers' goals. Although at one point they flirted with coercion by threatening a strike, they ultimately withdrew the threat in favor of a more positive strategy. Their use of noncooperation, although forceful, was not destructive.

The case also shows that even in conflicts outside the home the desire for harmony can prevail over narrow expressions of the instinct for self-protection. Personal relationships counted for much in the solution to this case: the workers needed Mason to show an appreciation for the quality of their work, and he needed an indication that they respected him as a true successor to his father. Even if Mason chooses not to stay with the company, the incident will have affirmed the importance of harmony and quality in the company's collective life. These are two virtues that are important for the doing of business anywhere, as Mason no doubt will discover even if he attempts to make a go of selling office furniture on his own.

♣ Case #3:
A Lonely Decision

Central Issues: Whether to take a moral stand; and whether to let one's personal life be made a public issue

Opponents: *Sarah v. Herself*

Principles at Stake: Honesty; pride in oneself; moral courage; the need to be effective in one's position

Attempted Resolution: Sarah decides that she can fight publicly for a position that concerns her personally without revealing her personal concern.

Sequence of events:

STAGE 1: The emergence of the conflict. The issue begins to surface during Sarah's last year in seminary, when she is looking forward to ordination in the ministry of the United Methodist Church. The Methodists have not ordained many women—although they are not opposed to it in principle, as the Roman Catholic church and some Protestant denominations are—and Sarah feels that her ordination will be a positive symbol of what the role of women in the church can be, as well as a challenging step in her own career. It is an important year for Sarah's professional development, and she is charged with excitement.

It is also a significant year in her personal life. For several years she has had a close relationship with Ted, a graduate student in architecture; but now that liaison has begun to crumble, and she finds that the solace she receives from her roommate, Karen, becomes as important to her as her friendship with Ted had been.

The intimacy culminates in a sexual involvement that catches Sarah by surprise but does not threaten her. In fact, it seems so natural and comfortable that she wonders whether her basic sexual orientation may be toward other women rather than toward men.

At first Sarah regards this as a private matter to be worked out by herself, or at most between herself and Karen. But a potential problem looms on the horizon: the matter of ordination.

It seems that although the Methodist Church is quite willing to accept women into its ministry, it does not extend the same hospitality to those who "condone the practice of homosexuality," for the church regards it as "incompatible with Christian teaching."[1] Sarah is not quite sure whether this applies to her, and the wording of the church's regulations are sufficiently ambiguous that she is not certain that it really prevents her or anyone else from being ordained. But the mere mention of the church's ruling makes her shudder. So do press reports that a national official in the church's women's division has been fired for admitting her lesbian relations. The tension inside Sarah mounts.

STAGE 2: *Search for Truth.* Sarah feels that she is in a quandary. On the one hand, she does not want to jeopardize her goal of ordination, toward which she has been working for several years, or to complicate it with a campaign for the right of sexual preference. On the other hand, she is proud of who she is, and feels a moral obligation to stand up for her rights and those of others who have been oppressed for whatever reason, including their sexual interests. She feels that the church is forcing her to make a choice between being a troublemaker and being dishonest, and that makes her angry.

While she is puzzling over her predicament, Sarah seeks out a trustworthy official in the church. She wants to know the basis of the church's stand, and whether there is any truth in it.

The official obliges by presenting her with what he regards as the biblical evidence for the church's position, but to Sarah it seems shaky at best, especially in view of the Bible's tender portrayals of the relationships between David and Jonathan, and Ruth and

Naomi. Moreover, she asks, doesn't the church teach that all who enter into its ministry are in some way sinners? If the church regards her as sinful, shouldn't it tolerate her as much as any other fallible human?

The church official explains to Sarah that the church's view of this matter is similar to its view of bank robbery: it is willing to ordain those with a predilection toward robbing banks, as long as they do not plan to commit or advocate the crime.

To Sarah this is cold comfort. She feels it is unfair for the church to label as a crime the sweetest friendship she has known, or to so label the sexual events that symbolize it.

Sarah decides that she respects nothing in the church's position, except perhaps the church's right to take a stand on a moral issue, even if it chooses wrongly. So again she is turned back on herself: if she is not ready to abandon her plans for ordination over this issue, how can she enter the ministry with integrity? After a great deal of soul-searching, she finally arrives at this conclusion: she will not make any public statement about her own sexual involvements, but after ordination she will vigorously fight to persuade the church to change its stand.

STAGE 3: *The campaign for acceptance.* Sarah herself is the only person she has to convince of the viability of this resolution, for it need not affect anyone else. Sarah discusses the solution with Karen, whose own position would not be threatened by disclosure, and Karen encourages Sarah to make whatever decision seems right for herself.

At first the decision to be silent seems to be the right one. It will allow Sarah to go on with her studies and plan for ordination without being burdened with the additional complications of having to explain and defend her sexuality. Especially since she feels so tentative about it herself, and so unsure about how it will affect her life later on, this seems the right path.

Still, she has trouble sleeping. One voice inside tries to comfort her, and commends her for making a mature decision and having the patience to take one step at a time. The other voice is less soothing. It uses words such as "cowardice" and "social apathy." This voice reminds her that she has always been honest, always a crusader, always ready to stand up for someone who is oppressed. To ignore the issue now will not cause it to go away, the voice reminds her. And if she does bring it up later, won't people wonder why she said nothing at ordination?

It is this second voice that persists through the night. When Sarah recounts her sleepless internal conversation at the breakfast table the next morning, this voice dominates. Karen asks her how the other candidates for ordination feel about the issue—whether any of them have to struggle with it. Sarah confesses that she doesn't know, and in fact had never thought to ask any of them about it.

Later in the day she contacts a number of her fellow ministerial candidates. Without revealing her own situation, she presents them with the church's stance and asks for their opinion. Most of them know about the issue, she discovers, and the overwhelming majority feel that the church has handled it badly. Many agree with Sarah that the church's underlying moral position in this matter is simply wrong. A few of them admit to sexual involvements of the sort that the church would not condone, and whisper to Sarah that privately they too are somewhat scared.

Sarah decides to act. She forms a small group composed of those with whom she has spoken. They call themselves Seminarians for an Honest Ordination, and circulate a petition expressing concern over the church's position on not ordaining those with wayward sexual preferences. To their surprise and pleasure, it is signed by the majority of the candidates for ordination in their region of the United Methodist church.

STAGE 4: The outcome. The time has come for the church's annual conference, the event that will culminate with the ordination of the new clergy, and Sarah is there with the Seminarians for an Honest Ordination, carrying a picket sign and handing out leaflets. It is a matter of some embarrassment to the leaders of the conference, who call for a closed session to air the issue.

All the ordained clergy of the region crowd into the closed room to hear Sarah and her colleagues argue against what she describes as a dogmatic and immoral position on the church's part. Her accusations are met with countercharges from some of the more conservative clergy, but ultimately cooler heads prevail, and the bishop, who does not welcome press coverage of this issue, points out that no one has actually breached the letter of the law as the church has stated it. No one has directly condoned the practice of homosexuality. The candidates are free to quibble over church policy as much as they wish, he explains, but as long as no evidence has been presented that they are not of "unquestionable moral character and genuine piety," as the regulation puts it, their ordination need not be delayed.[2]

At this point a particularly adamant church leader points accusingly at Sarah and says that he would indeed like to question her moral character. Does she, he wants to know, "condone homosexual practices"? Sarah, without quite knowing what is meant by that, responds that her private life is indeed private, and that that is precisely the issue their group defends: the right of clergy to be human and to share their moments of intimacy with whomever they choose, without being hounded by the church. The bishop intercedes, confident that no evidence of wrongdoing has been offered. He adjourns the meeting and calls for the ordination to commence, Sarah and all.

Comments:

This case involves two levels of conflict: one internal to Sarah and one internal to the church. In fact, a critical breakthrough in Sarah's understanding of her dilemma occurred when she realized the dual dimensions of the issue: that what she thought of as her problem was also the church's. The latter problem was never really resolved, for although the Seminarians for an Honest Ordination were allowed to make their point, church policy was not changed. The ultimate outcome might have been considerably less pleasant if Sarah had acknowledged what the church had forbidden: condoning the practice of homosexuality. At that point, the seminarians would have had to change their tactics and perhaps take the case to a different body, such as the church's national council of bishops or the press or even the courts.

At the other level, the internal one, the conflict was resolved more satisfactorily. Inner strife often seems to demand a harmonious resolution in a way that outer conflict does not, since few people want to live with an unresolved conflict buzzing in their heads, and this instance was no exception. But such an inner resolution is not always easy to achieve in a Gandhian way. When one is faced with several possible outcomes, it is very tempting to opt for the solution that promises the least in the way of further trouble. This is precisely the direction in which Sarah leaned in the initial stages of the conflict.

Her assessment of the truthful and untruthful aspects of both sides of the issue looked something like this:

Position of Silence	*Position of Disclosure*
1. Patience	1. Siding with oppressed
2. Effectiveness in one's ministry	2. Active social concern
3. Passive social concern	3. Delight in being thought a rebel
4. Fear of being stereotyped	4. Honesty
5. Disdain of the role of moral hero	5. Courage

Initially she tried to form a resolution by putting together her need to be an effective leader and her social concern (although the social concern would be actively expressed only after ordination). She rejected some of the negative motivations, such as the desire to be a rebel and a moral hero. The only problem was that this initial solution did not cover all of the aspects involved. It neglected her truthful need to be honest and courageous and morally committed, and these needs kept pursuing her.

Ultimately what kept her initial solution from working was her own strong sense of integrity. She was obeying what Gandhi once described as the "duty to respect and understand oneself."[3] The very notion of personal integrity implies the honoring of various aspects of one's own character, and before Sarah could achieve this she had to allow the various sides within herself to do battle.

This was a painful process, and the final solution left some ragged edges. In the end, her militant, open self and her careful, conservative self could not be totally at peace with each other. But she had begun to accommodate these differing sides of her personality and move closer to an integration of them. She was able to take a stand and to accept ordination at the same time.

Furthermore, the solution enabled her to raise an important issue of church policy, and it encouraged her to cultivate a new role, perhaps a new identity for herself: that of leadership in issues of social importance. In being open to a Gandhian resolution to the conflict inside her, Sarah was unwittingly opening herself to the risk that all Gandhian fighters face—the risk that in the course of fighting they may themselves be obliged to change.

❧ Case #4:
A Peaceful End to
Irish Terrorism

Central Issue: The political future of Northern Ireland

Opponents: *The Catholic IRA v. the Protestant Unionists* (and *the governments of Ireland v. the government of Great Britain*)

Principles at Stake: The ability of two groups who live in the same region to determine their own political identities, to be free from violence, and to be fairly governed

Attempted Resolution: The Good Friday Agreement, which established an end to violence, protected the interests of both Catholics and Protestants, and set up institutional relationships between them and among the governments of Northern Ireland, the Republic of Ireland, and Great Britain

Sequence of Events:

STAGE 1: The emergence of the conflict. In the broadest sense the troubles between Catholics and Protestants in Ireland began in the twelfth century with the Anglo-Norman invasion, which staked a claim for English rule on Irish soil. The conflict in Northern Ireland itself began several centuries later with the English establishment of the Plantation of Ulster in 1610. Choice land was given to new settlers, most of whom were Scottish Presbyterians. Dispossessed Irish Catholics tried to rebel in 1641 but were soon defeated. Their resentment over privileges given to the Protestant Scottish settlers has festered ever since.

As long as Ireland was part of Great Britain the status quo remained more or less unchallenged. But when Ireland demanded independence from Britain in the late nineteenth and early twentieth centuries, the Protestant community in Northern Ireland became worried. They feared that Irish home rule would put in power in Dublin a pro-Catholic government that would discriminate against them. Some feared the worst: that Protestants would be driven from the region that for several centuries they had come to call their home.

By 1912, when Protestant activists saw that Ireland's independence was inevitable, they argued for partition of the country, giving Northern Ireland a separate political status that would allow it to remain allied with the British union. Some of the most militant Protestants formed the Ulster Volunteer Force, an armed militia prepared to oppose by force any scheme that would make Northern Ireland part of an independent Irish state.

In the meantime the slow progress towards Irish independence had begun to inflame militant Catholics throughout Ireland. In 1918 the Irish independence party, Sinn Fein, swept all of the Irish constituencies except the Protestant North. In the following year an Irish Republican Army began a guerilla war for independence from Britain.

In 1921 the Irish Free State was created. This independent state had dominion status like Canada, but in every other way it was an independent Ireland. At the same time the Protestant section of the island was partitioned off and the state of Northern Ireland was formed. It continued to be ruled by London as a part of the British union. Protestants were in a majority in the new Northern Ireland, but a sizable population of Catholics also lived within the region. The Catholics soon complained that they were discriminated against in housing and employment and that local government boundaries were drawn to insure Unionist control over all areas of Northern Ireland, even the ones in which Catholics predominated.

A Civil Rights Association was created by Northern Irish Catholics in 1967. They were encouraged in part by the success of the moment led by Martin Luther King, Jr. for civil rights in the United States. A conciliatory Prime Minister of Northern Ireland, Terence O'Neill, was for a time open to the Catholics' concerns. But he was replaced by a hard-line regime intent on crushing what it regarded as a Catholic insurrection. In 1969 the brutal suppression of peaceful civil rights marchers helped to galvanize public opinion among Catholics. Civil rights advocates increased their protests and their demands. Counter-demonstrations were organized by the Protestant Reverand Ian Paisley and his Unionist supporters. The "troubles" of Northern Ireland had begun.

STAGE 1a: The escalation of violence. Violence erupted in the summer of 1969 in the Bogside area of the city of Londonderry (Derry) between Irish nationalist Catholics and Unionist Protestant marchers celebrating the anniversary of a historical Protestant victory over Catholics. This "Battle of the Bogside" in Londonderry was soon replicated by a similar clash in Belfast. British troops were brought in to give support to the Northern Irish police, thereby directly implicating the British government in the struggle.

In the Protestant community, the old Ulster Volunteer Force was revived to defend itself against what it imagined to be a Catholic insurrection. Pressure mounted within the Catholic community for the IRA to take a more aggressive, militant stance. In 1969 the Belfast Brigade of militant Catholics rejected what it regarded as the moderate position of the regular IRA and created its own separate "Provisional" IRA. A Provisional Sinn Fein was also created in 1970 to be the political party of the dissident militant Catholics of Northern Ireland.

By 1971, therefore, the stage was set for violent confrontation. Both Protestant and Catholic sides had taken extreme positions and formed paramilitary groups capable of violent actions. It was a time when astute leadership might have defused the confrontation. Alas, leaders on both sides took the hard line, and violence escalated.

On August 9, 1971, the government of Northern Ireland adopted a preemptive action policy and began rounding up Catholic activists it regarded as potential terrorists. The government held them in jail without charges. Within hours, rioting and shooting broke out in the Catholic neighborhoods of Belfast and adjacent towns. The government, rather than retreating from its hard line, pressed on, declaring a war on terrorism.

The massive roundup and internment of suspected IRA supporters continued. The prisoners were held without charges, and were beaten and tortured in an attempt to elicit information. They were forced to lie spread-eagle on the floor with hoods over their heads, and were subjected to disorienting electronic sounds.

The government's attempt to end the violence by harshly treating those it suspected of perpetrating violence was an approach that backfired. The Catholic community united even more solidly behind the insurgency, and the violence mounted. Later the home minister who sanctioned the crackdown admitted that the government's approach was "by almost universal consent an unmitigated disaster."

The violence of the early seventies reached a climax on what came to be called "Bloody Sunday"—January 30, 1972. A peaceful protest march against the internment of Catholic activists turned ugly, and British troops fired on the crowd. Thirteen civilian Catholics were killed. The Catholic community responded with a firestorm of angry reprisals, and Bloody Sunday was a recruitment boost for the IRA. At the same time, it fueled the recruitment efforts of Irish Unionists.

Bloody Sunday marked the beginning of a spiral of violence. Tit-for-tat acts of terrorism became a routine affair. The British embassy in Dublin was burned, British soldiers were attacked, police stations were bombed, and individual Catholics and Protestants were captured by opposing sides and sometimes hideously tortured and killed. Despite attempted cease-fires and overtures of negotiations from the IRA, the violence continued.

STAGE 2: The search for a resolution. By the mid-eighties it appeared that there was no easy way out of what had become a bitter, violent, intractable confrontation, with waves of terrorism from both sides. But the seeds of peace that had been planted in the ill-fated Sunningdale agreement of 1974 began to take root and grow again. In the Anglo-Irish Agreement of 1985, negotiated by Britain's Margaret Thatcher and Ireland's Garret FitzGerald, Ireland recognized Britain's rights over Northern Ireland. Britain, in turn, agreed to have Irish consultation regarding the Catholic minority in the region.

The Anglo-Irish Agreement was emphatically rejected by both sides in Northern Ireland itself: the Unionists and IRA alike saw it as a sell-out. The Reverand Ian Paisley, a Unionist leader, called on God to "take vengeance" on Margaret Thatcher, whom he described as a "wicked, treacherous, lying woman." Again the violence returned.

STAGE 3: The campaign for acceptance. In 1988 an internal dialogue began to take place within the Catholic side, between John Hume, a moderate who had been part of the Northern Ireland Civil Rights movement, and Sinn Fein leader Gerry Adams. Hume persuaded Adams that the British did not have a long-range plan to control Northern Ireland, that the Unionists had to have a face-saving exit strategy in whatever agreement was forged, and that any agreement would have to include directly the leaders of both Catholic Republicans and Protestant Unionists. When Hume was criticized for talking with the militant Adams, he said he did not care "two balls of roasted snow" about such criticism.

Other conversations were being held behind closed doors with representatives of the Provisional IRA, the Unionists, and the British and Irish governments. On December 15, 1993, the Downing Street Declaration announced that Britain had no "selfish strategic or economic interest in Northern Ireland." This persuaded Adams that a direct negotiation with the Unionists was possible, and in 1994 the Provisional IRA proclaimed a unilateral cease-fire. Less than two years later, frustration with a lack of progress in negotiations led to the end of the cease-fire and new terrorist bombings in London.

In 1995, to break the stalemate, an outside commission headed by former U.S. Senator George Mitchell was invited to help broker the peace talks. Initially the talks were unsuccessful and both sides broke down into mutual recriminations. In 1997 a new British government led by Tony Blair renewed the negotiations and again a cease-fire was proclaimed.

Mitchell returned to take part in eight months of intensive negotiations. They involved both the Irish and British governments and eight political parties on both Catholic and Protestant sides of the Northern Irish divide. Agreement was reached on April 10, 1998—a day that happened to be Good Friday, the Christian holiday that precedes Easter.

STAGE 4: The outcome. The Good Friday Agreement is a remarkable document in that it attempted to provide structural resolutions to several different problems at the same time. To solve the problem of public mistrust and insecurity brought on by years of violence, the Agreement set up human rights and equality commissions. It also provided the early release of political prisoners, required the decommissioning of paramilitary weapons, prescribed reforms of the criminal justice system and the policies of policing in Northern Ireland, and supplied funds to help the victims of violence. The Agreement also addressed the problems of governing Northern Ireland fairly, proposing a new division of powers and providing ways to facilitate relations among Northern Ireland, the Republic of Ireland, and Great Britain.

The Good Friday Agreement was an ambitious undertaking, and amazingly it has largely succeeded. The first election, on June 25, 1998, created a 108-member assembly with the largest Unionist party and the largest Republican party almost equal in size. The Protestant Unionist leader David Trimble was elected first minister.

Yet the road to peace has not been entirely smooth. The issue of decommissioning the arms of paramilitary units, especially those associated with the IRA, continued to be a problem. David Trimble resigned his post on July 1, 2001, in protest over the IRA's persistence in keeping its armament. By the end of the year, however, the Provisional IRA agreed to a decommissioning process and Trimble resumed his leadership—though not with full Unionist support.

Some of the most militant Unionist groups—including the supporters of Reverend Ian Paisley—have never cooperated with the peace process, and continue to resist any accommodation of those whom they regard as former terrorists. Extreme elements on the Catholic side—among them a group calling itself the "Real IRA"—also have shown their displeasure, in some cases violently.

In 1998 the Nobel Prize for Peace was jointly awarded to the Catholic leader John Hume and the Protestant leader David Trimble. They were commended for "their efforts to find a peaceful solution to the conflict in Northern Ireland." The Reverend Ian Paisley, archenemy of his fellow Unionist David Trimble and a fierce critic of the peace process, called the Nobel award "a bit of a farce."

Comments:

Though extremists like Paisley were not satisfied, the Good Friday Agreement marked a milestone in the modern history of conflict resolution. It is one of the few recent examples in which a violent confrontation marked with vicious acts of terrorism has been brought to a peaceful resolution. For this reason it provides a model for dealing with terrorism in a Gandhian way. Though it is sometimes said that violent tactics must be used when peaceful ones do not work, the Northern Ireland case shows that often the opposite is true: peaceful methods can succeed when violent means fail.

The British government and the paramilitary forces on both the Unionist and IRA sides found themselves in a situation similar to many violent confrontations. Their positions had been staked out in extreme and uncompromising terms and the methods used by all sides were so harsh as to be virtually unforgivable. Ultimately they were able to break through this impasse by employing several basic Gandhian techniques, including the following:

1. *Seeing the other side as varied and flexible.* When the British began to open lines of communication to the radical leaders on both sides, they began to break through the we-they attitude that vexes most hostile confrontations. Each side began to become aware that the options were more open than the extreme positions might suggest.

2. *Not responding to violence in kind.* Initially there was a tit-for-tat response to every terrorist incident. In the years preceding the agreement, however, leaders on all sides were more prudent. The cease-fires—including unilateral cease-fires by the IRA—were critical in helping to break the spiral of violence.

3. *Letting moderate voices surface.* A crucial moment in the process began on the Catholic side when the relatively moderate leader, John Hume, engaged in a series of conversations with the more radical leader, Gerry Adams. Once the spiral of violence had been broken and neither side felt under siege, there was room for moderate voices to surface within the warring camps.

4. *Isolating radical voices.* The peace negotiators did not try to change what could not be changed. They did not waste their time trying to reason with the Reverend Ian Paisley, for instance, who had opted out of the process on his own. Increasingly, extremists such as Paisley appeared isolated and out of touch with the more moderate public sentiment.

5. *Setting up structures of trust and communication.* The Good Friday Agreement was the capstone of the peace process and set up structures that allowed trust and mutual respect to develop. It was useful to have an outsider—former U.S. Senator Mitchell—play a mediating role in negotiating these agreements, providing an impartial framework for two sides that had been deeply mistrustful of one another.

Peace in Northern Ireland was not inevitable. There were certainly enough extremists to continue the struggle, as the actions of the so-called Real IRA and militant Unionists indicated. Mistrust, humiliation, and hatred lingered for many years after the Good Friday accord.

What persisted in the Northern Ireland peace process was the vision that the future need not be dictated by the past. A few stalwart political leaders were able to discard their old assumptions and plunge forward into the uncharted waters of peace. They led the way for more moderate stances to follow.

There is no assurance that the peace will last forever. Violence may again return to that troubled part of Ireland. Yet for a time the hope and trust associated with the sacred day of Good Friday seem to have given Protestants and Catholics alike the sense that a life together in Northern Ireland is possible after all.

✿ Case #5:
A Tragic Resistance

Central Issue: Survival

Opponents: *The Warsaw Ghetto v. the Nazi Regime*

Principles at Stake: The right to live, and to do so in dignity and freedom

Attempted Resolution: Attempt of Jews to use active resistance to oppose the brutality of the Nazis.

Sequence of Events:

STAGE 1: The emergence of the conflict. Before World War II, the Jewish community in Warsaw was one of the largest and most lively in Europe. It enjoyed a rich cultural and intellectual life, and possessed considerable economic power. Some 10 percent of the Polish population was Jewish, and Warsaw was one of its major centers.

There were tensions, however, between the Jews and the Gentiles in Warsaw, as there had been throughout Europe for centuries. Polish anti-Semitism was, in part, a vestige of old Christian animosities against the Jews, particularly in Europe. This ancient religious vendetta colored the speech of some of Christianity's most prominent leaders, of whom Martin Luther is an unfortunate example.

In the eighteenth and nineteenth centuries, a new force emerged —secular nationalism—which turned out to be even more hostile toward Jews than Christendom. The inner-directed, isolated, and traditionalist Jewish community was an anomaly in modern Europe; yet its economic strength was respected and feared. Many East

European Jews were not allowed—or were unwilling—to become assimilated into the mainstream of European cultural life, although some were able to do so by sacrificing their ties to their own cultural heritage. To philosophers and politicians of the time, the Jewish situation was a "question," an intractable problem that seemed to give the lie to the supposed homogeneity of modern secular nationalism.[1]

The existence of a pariah community such as the Jews provided a convenient scapegoat for Hitler and his National Socialists, who transformed anti-Semitism from prejudice to state policy. The articulation of that policy emerged by degrees, however, and it was not until after 1940 that Hitler enforced his "final solution" to the "Jewish question" on a mass scale; six million—roughly two out of every three—European Jews perished.

STAGE 2: Search for Truth. The Jews in Warsaw watch the events of the early 1930s in neighboring Germany with rising alarm. It is not until 1939, however, when Hitler's armies march across the border and invade Poland, that they are placed in direct confrontation with the Nazi regime.

But they have trouble finding out the truth about what is going on around them. The Nazi regime cloaks its affairs in secrecy, masking its policies by first stating one thing and then the other. From the outset of the Nazi occupation, the Germans treat the Jews as outcasts, impounding their shops and money, closing synagogues, and placing restrictions on their travel. In 1940, when the community is confined to a walled ghetto, the strictures become even more severe; then the tragic "deportations" begin. Even then, few have any certain information about the gruesome destination of those trips, and many of the others refuse to believe that such allegations can possibly be true.

Without being able to accept any information with certainty, it is difficult for the Jewish leadership to formulate any clear policy. Even though they have some information about the fate of the German Jews, that news is garbled, and the worst that is to befall the Jews in Germany, as elsewhere, is yet to come. All they know for certain is that the Nazi regime has embarked on a deliberate policy of racial exclusion, that it is determined in some way to destroy the Jewish community in Europe, and that many lives are imperiled as a result.

What can they do? What kind of truthful response to such perversion can be asserted? Jews in the Warsaw ghetto and throughout the world are debating just this question, and they are joined in their concern by sensitive observers in Eastern Europe and in many other parts of the globe.

Gandhi is one of these. As early as 1938, before the outbreak of the war, and before the most deadly of the mass executions had begun, he observes that "the German persecution of the Jews seems to have no parallel in history. The tyrants of old never went so mad as Hitler seems to have gone."[2]

Gandhi's advice is simple:

> If I were a Jew and were born in Germany, I would claim Germany as my home even as the tallest Gentile German might, and challenge him to shoot me or to cast me in the dungeon; I would refuse to be expelled or to submit to discriminating treatment.

And then he adds, somewhat patronizingly, that if they would accept their suffering voluntarily rather than forcibly, it would bring the Jews "an inner strength and joy."[3]

This suggestion, of course, is bitterly resented by many Jews. Hayim Greenberg, in an open letter to Gandhi in his journal *The Jewish Frontier*, writes that "a Jewish Gandhi in Germany, should one arise, could function for about five minutes, until the first Gestapo agent would lead him . . . directly to the gallows."[4] The Jewish theologian Martin Buber, whose own concept of "I - Thou" relationships in many ways parallels that of *satyagraha*, and who was previously greatly supportive of Gandhi's views, also parts company with Gandhi over this issue. An effective nonviolent stand can be taken even "against unfeeling human beings," claims Buber, but not against "a diabolic universal steam-roller" such as the Nazis.[5]

Gandhi holds firm. He responds that nonviolent resistance should be applied even if it is anticipated that the outcome will be tragic, for "sufferers need not see the result in their lifetime." Gandhi adds that he is "painfully conscious" that his suggestion "will give no satisfaction . . . to my many Jewish friends."[6]

STAGE 3: The futile campaign. No suggestion, neither Gandhi's nor any other, is satisfying to the Jews in the Warsaw ghetto in the early 1940s as they ponder their limited options. The truth of the matter seems clear enough: the Nazis are out to get them, and there is no room for compromise. There is not a shred of truth on the Nazi side. What can the Jews possibly do?

One choice is a sort of measured complicity. The Jews can agree to go along with some of the commands of the Nazis, hoping to avoid the worst of them. The other choice is resistance, individual or collective, violent or nonviolent.

The leaders of the ghetto's *Judenrat*, its governing body, are put in the dreadful position of having to carry out the commands of the Nazi occupation forces; they are even charged with the task of mustering the numbers required for each day's deportation. Usually the quotas specify the less productive and less respectable people, and Jewish leaders such as Adam Czerniakow negotiate with the Germans for fewer numbers, and attempt to protect the children.

In 1942 the pace of the deportations increases, and the Nazis, hoping to discourage any resistance to their orders, take a number of Jews hostage, including Czerniakow's own wife. In response to one order, he is able to bargain for a few exemptions, such as vocational students and husbands of working women, but he is not able to keep the Nazis from laying their hands on orphaned children. When these innocents are taken away, Czerniakow can no longer bear to deal with the Nazis in any way. He swallows the cyanide tablet that he has kept hidden, waiting for this awful occasion.[7]

Some people go sadly to the trains when ordered, wearing their prayer shawls with poignant dignity. Others refuse to go. In Warsaw there are 5000 like this, according to Nazi records.[8] Whether they resist passively or attempt to attack or insult their captors makes no difference: they are all instantly shot.

Collective resistance is employed by several underground groups. The resisters steal weapons and uniforms from the Germans, try to sabotage the Nazi communication system, and on at least one occasion in Cracow blow up a cafe frequented by German soldiers. Such measures are at first not always supported by the Jewish citizenry, who fear savage reprisals from the Nazis. Once most people begin to believe the situation is hopeless, however, the resistance groups receive greater support.

By the middle of 1942, only 45,000 of the original 350,000 Jews in the Warsaw ghetto remain, and their destiny is quite clear. Nazi patrols roam the streets, shooting Jews on sight. The resistance groups have solidified their support among the members of the ghetto by this time; they publish an underground newspaper, extend lines of comunication to the outside, and arrange for shipments of arms into the beleaguered ghetto. With encouragement and guidance from the resistance groups, the Jews who remain began to resist deportation collectively. German soldiers are forced to search them out and drag them to the trains in order to meet the quotas.

In Warsaw the resistance leaders begin preparing for a more active defense. In the last months of 1942 they are building up their cache of stolen and smuggled arms, and building bunkers behind which to fight.

The first test of their strength comes on January 18, 1943, when German troops surround the ghetto, and fighting begins. About 50 German soldiers are killed in the first skirmish, and for three days the deportations are halted, and the troops turn back.

The resistance forces are heartened, and their numbers grow enormously. With solid support from the ghetto community, they consolidate their control. They hold their own trials, accusing and executing some of the Jews who were Nazi accomplices. Several months go by, and it almost appears as if their attempts at resistance will succeed.

In the predawn hours of April 19, 1943, however, the German troops again surround the ghetto, and demand that the Jewish resistance forces surrender. They refuse to do so, and at daybreak the SS troops enter with tanks, rapid-fire guns, and 2000 soldiers.

The Jews fight back. Their home-made incendiary bombs blow up the tanks and destroy many of the rapid-fire guns. By sunset 200 German soldiers are killed. The Nazis retreat, leaving the ghetto still in the hands of the Jewish resistance.

That night happens to be the first Seder ushering in the Jewish festival of Passover. It is celebrated with a special but anxious fervor, punctuated by the distant sound of German guns.

For five days the small Jewish enclave holds off the invading forces, setting land mines to destroy troop trucks and tanks. In one instance the Jewish resisters are able to demolish one third of a German unit. From the rooftops they fly the red-and-white flag of Poland and the blue-and-white Jewish banner. After years of having endured unparalleled oppression and death, they are able to fight back and do so effectively. Their hopes and spirits are high.

STAGE 4: The outcome. This feeling does not last long. In the end, the Germans recall their troops and burn the ghetto down. In some instances the fires are started by the Nazis' anti-aircraft artillery shells; in other instances the fires are set deliberately. The ghetto becomes a storm of fire, and on May 8 the SS troops surround what is left of the headquarters of the Jewish resistance. About a hundred Jewish leaders are inside, and when the Germans begin to break through their final defenses, most of the resisters kill themselves in a mass suicide.

A few of the resisters manage to escape, but only a tiny fraction of the original total. An overwhelming number suffer the fate of 90 percent of Poland's Jews under Nazi occupation: they are destroyed. Hitler's policy of genocide has largely succeeded.

Comments:

For an unarmed and ill-prepared minority such as the Jews of Warsaw, perhaps no strategy could have succeeded against an opponent so powerful and so evilly single-minded as the Nazis. Thus the issue seems scarcely to be whether a Jewish Gandhi could have been successful in conflict with the Germans. All we can ask is whether *satyagraha* was attempted in some measure, or whether it could have been, and whether it had anything positive to offer in what was otherwise one of the most dismal chapters in history.

If we were looking for the Gandhians in this episode, whom should we choose—those who acceded to the Nazis' orders? They were certainly nonviolent, but because of their complicity in untruth, perhaps we should regard them as having forfeited their own principles. They may even have unwittingly helped to provide the occupying Germans with a certain legitimacy.

Yet the situation was extreme, and you may well feel that the terror in which they lived justified their behavior. In a situation in which violence is already occurring, after all, one of the prime Gandhian objectives is to diminish its level. Perhaps, you might say, they could have accomplished this by pretending to comply with Nazi orders and then evading them, delaying their execution long enough for some of the victims to escape. Many Jewish leaders at the time, in fact, felt that this was the only sensible choice, fearing that a more overt resistance would cause more violence than it prevented.

Gandhi's advice in these circumstances, however, was to resist, and the various attempts at Jewish resistance can be analyzed as a sort of *satyagraha* under stress. In his letters to the Jews, Gandhi strongly suggested that this resistance should be nonviolent, even if the resisters had to sacrifice their lives in order to make it so. But in other contexts Gandhi said that conditions could be so extreme that those who stood for truth were faced with the necessity of choosing between violent resistance and none at all. Gandhi said that in these cases "vengeance is any day superior to passive and helpless submission."[9]

Gandhi's concept of *tapasya*—the renunciation of self-interest, including the natural desire for personal safety—did not sanction passive self-destruction. Although he might have revered the conviction of the Buddhist monks who immolated themselves in Saigon during the Vietnam war as a protest against the fighting, it is unlikely that Gandhi would ever have followed their lead. One could hardly imagine a Gandhian masochist either, even though during the salt *satyagraha* in 1930 line after line of Gandhians allowed themselves to be beaten by the armed police without resisting, and Gandhi himself undertook fasts in which he expressed his "willingness to perish."[10]

Yet it is clear that such actions are justifiable only if they serve to purify the Gandhian actors and effect some moral response in the hearts of those who cause them harm. In the case of the Jews in Warsaw, neither of these was the case. Their situation was more analogous to an instance of rape, which Gandhi offered as a hypothetical case in which a violent response could be justified. In such cases, he felt, resistance is more honorable than inaction, even if the resistance has to be physically coercive.

Considering the dire circumstances in which the Warsaw resisters found themselves, Gandhi certainly would have approved of the courage that they demonstrated by choosing the course they did, and he might well have applauded their spirit of resistance, even though the outcome was tragic. They did employ violence, but in many other ways the uprising was similar to one of Gandhi's nonviolent campaigns: the resisters attempted to mobilize the community, build up its strength, resist capitulating to the untruth of deportation, and provide for an alternative form of government. There was no need to assess which side was right and which was wrong, for the indiscriminate brutality of the Nazi forces branded them at the outset as untruthful to the core. And squarely on the Jewish side of the struggle was the most fundamental and truthful demand that can be made: the right to live.

The Jewish resistance was an almost perfect *satyagraha* campaign, therefore, except for its violence. If less militant means had been used to halt the tanks and troops—setting up roadblocks and infiltrating the Nazi communications system, for example—the campaign would have fit the Gandhian model exactly. But in that event it is unlikely that the resisters could have held out for so long a time. Perhaps in the case of the Warsaw ghetto uprising we have the unusual situation where *satyagraha*, if it were to be waged at all, had to be waged violently.

In the end, although it heartened Jews throughout the world, the Warsaw resistance did not seem to have much impact on the Nazis. Violent resistance led to the same horrifying end that nonviolent resistance did: the Jews were destroyed. Their problem was not one of strategy but one of strength. They did not have the numbers, organization, or arms to launch any significant campaign, violent or not.

Gandhi frequently argued that *satyagraha* could be effective only when waged "from strength, rather than weakness."[11] The effectiveness of the Jewish resistance was certainly undermined by its weakness as a small, isolated minority community. Realizing this, many of the Warsaw resisters saw that their only hope for survival lay in developing alliances outside their own helplessly trapped enclave.

What would have been the most effective alliance, however, was never realized—one between the Polish Jews and prominent Polish and German Gentiles who could have influenced Nazi leaders. After all, the larger conflict at the time involved not only the Jews but the whole of European society, even the whole of Western society. The question of whether the untruth of Nazism should be allowed to continue affected them all. That is what the war was about, and perhaps a show of military force was necessary to subdue the force of the Nazis and the Axis powers. From a Gandhian point of view, however, many opportunities for nonviolent struggle against the lies of National Socialism slipped by before the violent struggle began.

Those Germans who saw the emergence of demonic repression against the Jews and allowed it to flourish unchallenged are particularly culpable. Although some German church leaders were actively opposed to the Nazi repression—the theologian Dietrich Bonhoeffer gave his own life in an abortive attempt on Hitler's—the churches were largely silent.[12]

The fundamental failure of *satyagraha* in this case, then, was not the inability of that brave but hopelessly outnumbered band of resisters to succeed at Warsaw, but the failure of others to speak out against the Nazis before they became such a virulent force. Perhaps it was incorrect to have described this case as a conflict between the Warsaw Jews and the Nazis. Perhaps the Jews were only victims in a larger conflict, the struggle against the falsity of National Socialism and its racist ideology. That struggle was waged in earnest much too late to save them and the many others whose lives were tragically sacrificed.

SECTION III:
SOME SMALL QUARRELS

❧ Conversations in the Mind

Even those of us who admire Gandhi and his ideas may occasionally be exasperated by his actions and question some of his concepts. And those who are less admiring may at this point in the discussion find aspects of Gandhian thought downright baffling. Are there are not moments when a bit of coercion can be justified for a righteous cause? And isn't it sometimes better to let our anger rage than to try to be so painfully kind and sensible? You may also question the possibility of coming to a real agreement with an opponent over what is the truth, and the feasibility of waging a moral struggle with a mammoth, impersonal organization.

In short, you may want to fight with Gandhi. It may be a major difference of opinion over fundamental assumptions or only a small disagreement over tactics, but Gandhi's challenges are not easily ignored. The importance of the issues and the certainty of his stand seem to demand some sort of response.

We haven't the real Gandhi to quarrel with, of course, but we can fight with his ideas the way we frequently respond to issues that puzzle us in our daily lives: we can play out the contrary positions in our minds. Fortunately, others have thought about these same issues and offered opposing viewpoints to Gandhi's. Some of these thinkers are among the most formidable minds of the past century, and in our own reflections we can juxtapose Gandhi's ideas to theirs.

In this section I will present several of these mental encounters the way I sometimes imagine them occurring: as conversations. The Gandhian position will be portrayed as if Gandhi were speaking, and the skeptical voices will be provided by three figures whose ideas sharply challenge Gandhi's, each in a different way. Karl

Marx, Sigmund Freud, and Reinhold Niebuhr had many concerns in common with Gandhi, and these mutual concerns provide the basis for debates with Gandhi about the use of violence and coercion, the expression of anger, the search for truth, and the potential for moral action in a modern, organizational world. I will use the actual words of Gandhi and the other thinkers, for the most part, in giving expression to their points of view.

Following these debates is an encounter of a different sort. This time Gandhi is his own opponent as the Gandhi of action faces the Gandhi of ideas. In a series of imaginary letters, Gandhi's theories are used as a framework for analyzing some of the events in Gandhi's life, and in return the active Gandhi tries to defend his deeds. As in the earlier dialogues, Gandhi's own words are used to present his position; the only difference this time is that Gandhi speaks both for and against himself.

In a Gandhian fight the goal is to find some resolution of differing perspectives on the truth, and there are moments in the conversations between Gandhi and his three adversaries when areas of resolution appear. But in most cases the differences are deep and not easily bridged. We will take up some of these issues later on, in the final chapter of this section.

✼ Issue #1:
Can Violence Ever Be Justified?

—GANDHI v. MARX

Central to the Gandhian approach is the notion that violence —or any sort of coercion, in the Gandhian view—cannot be allowed. Yet as we have just seen in our consideration of the Warsaw Ghetto, during times of social upheaval and struggles against massive political oppression, nonviolence may appear to be a luxury that few can afford. The issue is a burning one today around the world in places where people agonize over whether to use violence in their efforts at change.

Gandhi's advice in such cases would be to struggle nonviolently, but in the face of monstrous oppression is such advice foolhardy? Karl Marx (1818-1883) would have thought so. One of modern history's greatest strategists of social transformation, Marx saw society as locked in fundamentally violent struggles for power. In his view, any sort of effective change would have to be violent as well. It is this position of Marx's—so radically different from Gandhi's— that is to be the focus of their imaginary debate.

Gandhi and Marx never met in real life, of course. Marx was born half a century before Gandhi, and lived in a very different world. It is true that Gandhi arrived in London as a student scarcely six years after Marx had died there, but the cultural backgrounds of the two were poles apart. In temper and style they were equally opposed: Gandhi was an activist and an ascetic; Marx was an intellectual who lived modestly less because of choice than circumstance.

Yet they shared much. Both were concerned with what they saw as economic and political oppression brought about by an industrialized society. Both saw the modern world as dehumanizing, a circumstance that called for a radical analysis and an active effort for social change. Both were unabashed visionaries. The new societies they longed for were egalitarian communities, societies restructured to be in accord with what they conceived to be the naturally harmonious dispositions of ordinary human beings. Such basic instincts of trust and generosity, however, could fully emerge only with the demise of the dreary and despotic institutions of the day.

The major differences between Gandhi and Marx are to be found in their ideas about what is required to transform this imperfect world into a better one, and these differences are so significant that they color all other aspects of the comparison between them as well. Marx believed that unjust societies could change only when groups of oppressed people were able to seize power from the groups that exploited them. Gandhi's point of view, by contrast, was that any real transformation of this world into a better one had to begin with an inner change. It had to be a conversion of the heart, although Gandhi was not above using a little external encouragement to spur that change along. Gandhi's approach was ultimately personal, whereas Marx's was economic and political, and this difference reflects their profoundly different conceptions of human nature.

Gandhi and Marx also disagreed sharply on the use of violence as a tool for social change. This disagreement was far more than a question of strategy; it was so fundamental, in fact, that it colored almost everything they thought about the world. If they had ever met and talked, it would not have been long before the subject turned to social change and the use of violent means. Perhaps we could imagine them engrossed in conversation about just such matters at a pub or coffeehouse somewhere near the University of London, a neighborhood where each of them lived for many years.

GANDHI: It's just that you seem such a pleasant fellow, so concerned about the human condition—intellectually passionate, I suppose, but not the sort to advocate violence.

MARX *(with good humor):* I suppose I should take that as a compliment.

G: Indeed.

M: Well, you will be pleased to know that my goal in life is hardly the advocacy of violence. My aim is the abolition of self-alienation, the recovery of human nature, the return of humanity to a social being.[1]

G: Excellent. [Pauses.] But you also advocate violence.[2]

M: Not in every instance. There are countries—England and America, for instance—where the workers can attain their goals through peaceful means. But in most countries, the lever of our revolution must be force.[3]

G: "Must"?

M: There are times when we scarcely have a choice.

G *(frowning):* Oh, I think there is always a choice.

M: Certainly. We have a choice to do nothing or to do something.

G: Yes, and beyond that . . .

M *(interrupting):* You're getting the point. Beyond that there is the matter of choosing effective means.

G: That's not quite the point I had in mind.

M: I beg your pardon.

G: It seems to me that you've already chosen the means when you choose the goal, and in the case of a violent situation . . .

M *(interrupting again):* . . . you are forced to use violent means! You see, you do have the point after all.

G *(a bit warily):* What I had in mind was that violence breeds violence, and that if you use it in your struggle for change, the result will also have a violent tinge.[4]

M: Perhaps so, but your dictum holds true at the outset of a struggle as well as at the end. A violent situation naturally produces a violent response—in fact it requires it. It demands a force that can match and subdue the brutality that is there.

G: Well yes, in part. A violent situation must be met with strength. But that strength need not itself be violent.

M: I suppose not, if less extreme means are available and prove to be efficacious.[5] These might work well enough if your opponent is a manageable and not overly vicious sort. But if you are confronted with a whole social system built on violence, one in which violence is integrated into the very marrow of the state, that is another matter.[6]

G: By violence in this sense you mean . . .

M: I mean what you mean by violence: violating another person, not only physically, but causing him to be corrupted, lost to himself, alienated, and subjected to the rule of inhuman conditions.[7] Every act of exploitation does this, I'm sure you agree.

G: Of course. And it should be opposed.

M: Yes, destroyed. We agree. And if the whole social structure is irredeemable—violent and exploitative by its very nature—then you are left with no choice but to overthrow the political system that sustains the old institutions.[8]

G *(nodding):* It is sometimes necessary to supplant an unjust system with a totally new one . . .

M *(interrupting):* . . . and to use a strategic violence to bring it down. Again, we agree?

G *(puzzled over this turn in the argument):* We were fine up to the last, and then I'm afraid I lost you. Perhaps you should repeat your line of reasoning . . .

M: Let us find an example instead.

G: Fine. Would slavery do?

M: Slavery it is. The situation is utterly without moral redemption as far as I'm concerned.

G *(expansively):* Of course I would agree.

M: Slaves and their owners stand in constant opposition to one another.[9] But you are never going to sweet-talk your slave owners out of the arrangement, my friend, as long as there are enormous profits to be made. Now is that not a fact?

G: Most likely you are right.

M: Well then, something must be done.

G: Quite so. What do you suggest?

M *(sternly):* Well, since there is in fact an uninterrupted, albeit hidden conflict, it needs to surface in an open fight . . . [10]

G: Marvelous! I could not have put it better.

M *(continuing):* . . . in an uprising of some sort. Organize the slaves. Awaken their consciousness about the truth of their oppression. Create a positive program for change. If slaves and owners do not establish a revolutionary reconstruction of society they will all collapse in a common ruin![11]

G *(applauding):* Well said!

M *(taken aback):* Really, Mr. Gandhi. I'm surprised you are so approving!

G *(in an analytical mood):* An excellent solution, for the most part. Well done. Some small questions, however.

M: Yes?

G: What happens to the slave owners?

M: I don't know. They're put to work somewhere. Banished, maybe. Or taken out and shot.

G: Which?

M *(a bit annoyed):* I don't know. What difference does it make? Damn the slave owners.

G: Considerable difference. It makes all the difference in the world.

M *(trying to be agreeable):* Yes, you are right, it is not an inconsequential matter. But you do exaggerate. In the sweep of history, it hardly makes a "world" of difference, now does it? If we reeducate the landlords rather than killing them off, would that please you?[12]

G: Yes, very much.

M: Don't misunderstand. I don't mean to appear callous about peoples' lives, but we are not talking about family squabbles, we are talking about significant changes in world history: long struggles, a series of historic processes and transforming circumstances.[13] And you appear more concerned with the fate of a few despots than with the freedom of the masses of oppressed.

G: Not more than, but yes, concerned.

M: Your concern is touching. But it is not very realistic. If a million people were held in oppression by one maniacal despot, wouldn't the most charitable solution be to destroy that sole agent of terror?

G: It's not that I want to hide from the question, but I thought you earlier implied that most terror of this sort was institutionally imposed?

M: Quite so.

G: That being the case, no effective change will come about until that whole social order is changed.

M: Exactly. And that is what I am talking about: reconstructing society through effective means.[14] Strategically, by reversing the centers of power.

G *(exasperated):* Yes, yes . . . but there is more at issue here than finding the means for changing society, my friend. Your goal will be affected by your means.

M: The goal is socialism.

G: Especially if the goal is socialism. It is a beautiful word, socialism.[15] And I have the greatest admiration for the self-denial and spirit of sacrifice of those like you who are committed to social revolution.[16]

M: Then?

G: Then the problem is violence, as I have said. And the power of the state, even a socialist one, a power which I look upon with the greatest fear. Though it does good by minimizing exploitation, it does the greatest harm to mankind by destroying individuality.[17]

M *(heatedly):* Individuality! That phrase usually masks such bourgeois values! If by the "individual" you mean the slave owner, or even a middle class owner of property, these persons must indeed be swept out of the way, and made impossible.[18]

G *(testily):* I do mean these persons, and everyone else, for that matter. Freedom of the individual is at the root of all progress.[19]

M: Progress? That sounds more like an illusion. My dear Mr. Gandhi, by grasping after heaven you may lose it on earth. You are like those old Christians who neglected and despised politics, who chafed at the idea of seizing political power.[20]

G *(defensively):* Not so. I believe that the way to heaven, to truth, is through political action.

M: Effective political action.

G: Yes, effective action. I am not afraid to challenge a despot if necessary.

M: Then why should you fear a small moment of violence in the great drama of social transformation?

G: Because it affects that transformation. And when your adversary is the whole social order, as you have said so eloquently, your strategy must in some way involve every single soul in that society. So an effective change ultimately means . . .

M *(interrupting):* . . . transforming the social order, changing everyone's way of thinking.

G: Correct. This time, at least, you have anticipated my point.

M *(brightening):* Then you do agree! The ultimate form of transformation is a change of consciousness, a recovery of unalienated self-consciousness . . .[21]

G: . . . a change that comes about through understanding, yes. Through harmonizing opposing points of view.

M: Well, through education, certainly, and a dialectical synthesis between oppositions.

G *(trying to agree):* Yes, there is a sort of dialectic there.

M *(still enthusiastic):* And you would agree that this new consciousness can come only when old tyrants vacate their seats of power?

G: . . . well . . .

M: And you agree that that end can be attained, of course, only by forcibly ejecting them and overthrowing all other existing social conditions?[22]

G *(after a brief silence):* Well. We seem to be so near, yet so distant.

M *(after an equal pause):* Yes, perhaps so. Close and far. I suppose I disturb you because I, fearing injustice and the torpor of change, tolerate violence. And you, fearing injustice but also violence, tolerate a gradual change.

✣ Issue #2:
Can Anger Be True?
—GANDHI *v*. FREUD

When we confront our opponents, Gandhi advised, we should honor them and try to see their side. According to Gandhi, this may involve denying ourselves, accepting the brunt of whatever hostility occurs, and refusing to express anger—for Gandhi thought anger could be as violent and destructive as physical force. But is such self-denial always a healthy thing? And are there not instances when suppressing our anger would actually inhibit progress in resolving a conflict?

Gandhi would probably have resisted this line of questioning. The reason is that truth, in his view, is known only in conflict, and then only when each party is able to put its own views to one side long enough to see the larger picture. Emotions, from Gandhi's perspective, make for an ineffective fight. Yet fights are usually full of passionate and strongly stated feelings. Could Gandhi possibly have been wrong?

To challenge Gandhi on this matter we have summoned a master at questioning people about their motivations and intentions, someone who held a frame of reference for looking at humanity that was very different from Gandhi's—Sigmund Freud.

Freud lived from 1856 to 1939, so he and Gandhi could have met or corresponded, but they never did, and there is no indication that either was aware of the other in any special way. And for good reason: Freud, sitting in his study in Vienna, would probably have seen Gandhi as someone interested solely in political activity and social reform, ventures remote from his own. To Gandhi, Freud's pioneering explorations into the psychological aspects of neurology and his development of psychotherapy as a technique and a field of study would probably have seemed similarly arcane. Even today, in fact, some Hindus regard Freudian analysis as an idiosyncrasy of the West, based on assumptions about the self that have no currency in India. Gandhi showed no interest in psychotherapy; perhaps he shared such a view.

Yet Gandhi and Freud had more in common than either might have thought. The basic idea of psychotherapy is in some ways strikingly similar to that of *satyagraha,* for in both cases the aim is to struggle toward greater harmony by seeking higher levels of truth, and both Freud and Gandhi were committed to an honest search, stripped of illusions. Freud's arena was the mind. He attempted to uncover the compromises made between competing impulses within the unconscious. Gandhi's realm was a moral and social one. Yet he too was suspicious of easy accommodations with illusions and untruths.

Their approaches are described by Erik Erikson in *Gandhi's Truth* as "two corresponding methods of dealing with our instinctuality in a non-violent manner."[1] According to Erikson, psychoanalysis as it was practiced by Freud "amounts to a *truth method,* with all the implications which the word truth has in Satyagraha."[2] Erikson goes on to claim that this analogy between Freud and Gandhi is "a correspondence in method and a convergence in human values which may well be of historical, if not evolutionary, significance."[3]

Be that as it may, there is still much over which Gandhi and Freud might have disagreed, beginning with the notion of truth, a concept that was central to Freud's thought as well as Gandhi's. To Gandhi, the term was linked with the moral posture of nonviolence, the abolition of the will to harm; Freud, as we shall see, understood the matter differently. It is easy to imagine that if Gandhi and Freud had met, they might well have found themselves discussing just such an issue, perhaps in Freud's comfortable, book-lined study in Vienna.

FREUD: Perhaps I misunderstand. You disavow committing any act of violence—a most civil and commendable point of view. But do I understand correctly that you go further, and deny even the inclination to harm?

GANDHI: The desire to harm, yes.

F: But what do you mean by "the desire to harm"? You mean
     anger, do you not? Hatred, vengeance, wrath—what else would
     a desire to harm mean?

G: All of those things, I suppose. Yes. I couldn't imagine someone
     seriously setting out after truth and harboring such sentiments.
     Such a person should not be angry with anyone who has in-
     jured him; on the contrary, he will wish him well.[4] One should
     try to get rid of the destructive attitudes before one begins.

F: Well then, it's to be a lonely journey, isn't it?

G: I beg your pardon?

F: Your search for truth. You know, I can't imagine a single soul
     capable of what you are asking: to rid the psyche of anger.

G: I believe I said one should try. The absence of anger is the
     perfect state, to which one should aspire.[5] None of us can attain
     it all of the time. You mustn't sound as if I were calling for
     perfection.

F: It's not the extremity of your requirement that concerns me. It's
     not a problem of degree. It's the very idea of it—repressing
     anger. It seems antithetical to an honest search for the truth.

G: I suppose it depends on what one regards as honesty . . .

F   *(interrupting):* . . . or rather, what one regards as truth. Ideas
     are not the only things that express truth, you know. Feelings
     also can be terribly expressive. When you deny them, you keep
     them hidden from the conscious mind. You prevent the mind
     from dealing rationally with them and keeping them under con-
     trol.[6]

G: Well then, we should simply abandon them, shouldn't we?

F: If we could. But that's not easily done. If you simply repress an
     impulse, it doesn't disappear. It retains its energy even though
     you may have no memory of it.[7]

G: How vicious!

F: Precisely. A submerged emotion, such as the anger you dislike
     so much, may return in an even more virulent form, and prove
     itself victor in the end.[8] Better that it be released at the outset
     instead.

G: You make it sound virtuous to be unpleasant.

F: Not virtuous, but sometimes necessary. One has to express and channel the angers and aggressions, the passions and lusts.

G: Perhaps we shouldn't discuss lust . . .

F *(pursuing his point):* What we should discuss is your inability to take seriously the human emotions. Yours is a rather typical case of repression, if you don't mind my mentioning it—one frequently observed in the lives of saints and penitents.[9]

G *(pleased at the comparison):* Such company! Surely I don't belong.

F: You belong.

G: But I think you misinterpret me. I take feelings of anger quite seriously. That's why I feel that the animal nature must be dealt with. One must conquer it before one moves on to look for truth.[10]

F *(warming to the point):* But this animal nature, as you call it, is a real part of human nature. Our instincts are of two kinds: those which seek to preserve and unite, and those which seek to destroy and kill. Neither is less essential than the other; the phenomena of life arise from the mutually opposing action of both.[11] Both are quite real, wouldn't you agree?

G: Well, there is real and then there is Real.

F: I beg your pardon?

G: Although I think that it is "real" when we feel such hateful things, I also think that there are layers of reality in the human perception of them. Perhaps you would assent to that. And wouldn't you say that the most vital and essential part of ourselves, that truthful core, is the affirmation of life?[12]

F: Yes, in part. Libido. It is linked with those sexual feelings you find so embarrassing. But—and this is a curious thing—I find there is a death wish in us as well, also at the core. Of course, this feeling of anger or hatred is usually aimed at others, and is not normally a self-destructive sentiment.[13]

G: I beg to differ.

F: About what?

G: About that. I feel that violence is caused to the self by its very expression, no matter who the supposed target.

F *(defensively):* And I feel that even more violence is done to the integrity of our human character by hiding violent feelings, since they convey such potent, primordial truths.

G: But some things in human nature are not worth retaining. A feeling of violence, for example, is not and cannot be truthful. How could it be? It negates existence.

F *(trying to understand)*: Negates? But the feeling itself *is*. It exists. Don't you claim to base your notion of *satya* on a bedrock of reality?

G: On reality, yes. Not on the illusions of untruthful, animal sentiments.

F *(brightening)*: Aha. Now I begin to understand. It's your notion of reality that is causing us to disagree.

G *(puzzled)*: There is only one reality.

F: Only one, I agree. But yours is clouded with mysticism. It is, dare I say, religious—prescriptive rather than descriptive. You have an ideal notion of reality in mind, and in my opinion your hope that human aggressiveness and coercion will disappear is, like Marx's, an illusion.[14]

G: So it may be. And yours?

F *(caught off guard)*: My what?

G: Is your notion of reality so free from any taint of idealism?

F: Why yes, of course. Like all scientific quests, my effort is simply to know what is what. But I do believe that through the strengthening of intellect there can be a displacement of instinctual aims and a restriction of instinctual impulses.[15]

G: And beyond that?

F: Beyond that? Well, I suppose I harbor the hope that people can share emotional ties more than they have in the past. The structure of human society is to a large extent based on this.[16]

G: An admirably moral stand . . .

F *(interrupting to return the compliment)*: As is yours. On the whole, I appreciate your attempt to base morality on reason and honesty rather than on sheer sentiment and the dictates of dogma. But your idealization of nonviolence, I'm afraid, betrays a lurking altruism.

G: And I find your hopes for the moral efficacy of reason to be equally as touching. Some might call that an idealism too, you know.

F   *(hesitantly):* I myself might call it a . . . a Utopian expectation, this notion that the instinctual life can be subordinated to the dictatorship of reason.[17] But what else could possibly protect us from that terrible cloud that is suspended over us all—the curse of war?[18]

G   *(somewhat surprised):* Then you are, you are a . . .

F: Yes, I am a pacifist. I thought you knew. Like you and Einstein, the physicist, I find that my repudiation of war is not merely intellectual or emotional. It is fundamental to my nature. I have a constitutional intolerance for war.[19]

G   *(hurriedly agreeing):* Yes, nonviolence is the most fundamental law of life.

F   *(frowning):* Well, I wouldn't put it quite that way. I still think that as a general principle conflicts of interest between men are settled by the use of violence.[20] And there is no use trying to get rid of men's aggressive inclinations.[21]

G   *(throwing up his hands):* Then?

F: Then we can try to control them, and to integrate violence into the social order in a positive way, in the form of laws.[22]

G   *(shrugging):* The same logic would sanction war.

F: No . . . well, perhaps. There is a sort of dreadful logic to war.[23] My objection to war is more fundamental than that. It is because everyone has a right to his own life, because war puts an end to human lives that are full of hope, because it brings individual men into humiliating situations, because it compels them against their will to murder other men . . .[24]

G: So, despite all your reason and your science eventually you, like me, retreat to moral ground.

F: The main reason why we rebel against war is simply that we cannot help doing so. We are pacifists, you and I, for some fundamental organic reason. We are simply obliged to be.[25]

❧ Issue #3:
Is a Force of Love
Realistic?

—GANDHI v. NIEBUHR

One of the most attractive promises of Gandhi's scheme is that it will help you to be more effective in your fighting, not just more moral. *Satyagraha*, according to its supporters, actually works. It changes minds and brings about a peaceful resolution to conflict. Those who support the nonviolent way point to a long string of effective nonviolent campaigns, including the civil rights movement in America, labor movements throughout the world, and, of course, India's struggle for independence.

Gandhi's critics, however, are unimpressed. They credit these successes to coercion rather than conversion, and give a good reason for their belief: according to them, many opponents by their very nature are unable to be affected by moral suasion.

Organizational entities, they claim, are cases in point. In 1978, Kenneth Kaunda, the president of Zambia and a noted disciple of Gandhi's, renounced the nonviolent position he had followed for years as leader of his country's nationalist movement. In supporting the guerrilla freedom struggle in neighboring Zimbabwe, Kaunda made a fundamental discovery: that "the power which establishes a state, . . . maintains it, . . . and eventually overthrows it is violence."[1]

Kaunda's unhappy conclusion—that social power is based on coercion—is not so different from Thomas Hobbes' insight centuries earlier; and even Aristotle may be interpreted as saying the same thing. The point has been stated forcefully in our own century by

Reinhold Niebuhr (1892-1971), who placed it into a moral context. He developed an approach to ethics that takes into account the violent character of organizational power.

Niebuhr's conclusions were quite different from Gandhi's, but his moral and religious convictions were equally as strong, and for this reason he is a good opponent to debate the Mahatma on the issue of whether organizational power is inherently corrupt. Niebuhr was keenly aware of Gandhi's ideas and was, in fact, a pacifist himself for some time. The two never met, but Gandhi's ideas continued to be a point of reference for Niebuhr even after his own thinking moved away from pacifism and evolved into what came to be called Christian realism.

Niebuhr has been variously described as a political philosopher, a Christian theologian, a social activist, and a founder of the field of modern social ethics. He was also the architect of many of the liberal policies that gained wide acceptance in America in the Roosevelt years. George Kennan, referring to his circle of liberal Democrats, described Niebuhr as "the father of us all,"[2] and Arthur Schlesinger, Jr., praised him for giving "new strength to American liberal democracy."[3] More recently public figures as diverse as Jimmy Carter and Jeane Kirkpatrick, Ronald Reagan's ambassador to the United Nations, have utilized Niebuhr's ideas.

Niebuhr began his career in 1915 as a pastor in Detroit, where the dehumanizing effects of modern industrial capitalism made a deep impact on his social sensibilities. He looked to his own Protestant background for insights into the problem, and found them expressed best in a concept that many sophisticated Christians of his time tried to ignore: original sin. Relying on the neo-orthodox theology of Karl Barth and the ideas of Luther, Augustine, and Paul, Niebuhr developed an ethical perspective based on the notion that the human capacity for generosity and sacrificial love is always tainted by the inclination to be self-serving and even destructive.

Niebuhr's Christian realism does leave room for love and unselfishness in its otherwise harsh assessment of human nature, but largely on a personal level or through institutions set up for the purpose of administering justice. Most large political and economic organizations, Niebuhr thought, are projections of the most selfish impulses. There is nothing wrong with this, from Niebuhr's point of view, but because of their self-serving natures they can scarcely be expected to show altruism if left to their own devices; laws and regulations are necessary to control them. About all one can hope for in the morality of nations and large corporations is that laws can keep them from doing more evil than they otherwise might. With such forces held at bay, a decent if not perfect society may come about.

This point of view made a considerable impact on left-of-center political thought in America, especially during the Roosevelt era, when Niebuhr came to be called "the prophet to politicians."[4] And he did not just prophesy from his writing desk: Niebuhr had already become something of a political activist during his pacifist years. During that time he helped establish the Fellowship of Reconciliation, which continues to be the largest religious pacifist organization in the United States. Later he was involved in the Fellowship of Socialist Christians and was a founder of the Americans for Democratic Action, the Liberal party in New York, and the liberal Christian journal, *Christianity and Crisis,* to which he was a frequent contributor.

Niebuhr was involved in numerous campaigns for social justice throughout his life. He opposed what he considered to be the evils of capitalism and the oppression of dictatorships, both fascist and communist, while championing the rights of women and racial minorities. In his later years he strongly criticized America's involvement in Vietnam.

After the rise of Stalin and Hitler, Niebuhr became especially suspicious of what he regarded as sentimental approaches to combatting political evil; and he considered Gandhi's an obvious case in point. He addressed Gandhi directly in *Moral Man and Immoral Society,* published in 1932, and his remarks there form the basis for much that he says in the dialogue that follows. To my knowledge, Gandhi never responded to Niebuhr's initiative, but we can imagine him doing so. We might picture them chatting one afternoon in the comfortable living room of Niebuhr's apartment near Union Theological Seminary in upper Manhattan. Through the window they have a fine view of Riverside Park and the cliff-lined Hudson River beyond.

GANDHI: I'm curious about the fact that you gave up pacifism. What went wrong?

NIEBUHR *(with good humor)*: The world, basically.

G *(sympathetically)*: Oh?

N: Yes. I found that the things we like to depend upon for social hope are rather fragile things. Utopian dreams. You see, I used to believe in Marxism, and then there was Stalin. I used to believe in pacifism, and then there was the demonic power of Hitler . . .

G *(interrupting)*: You used to believe in yourself . . .

N *(agreeing and continuing)*: . . . and then I found that I have a great capacity for evil: a self-serving, unjust, aggrandizing, violent character.[5] We all do.

G: Goodness!

N *(dryly)*: Quite the contrary. [Brightening] Yet we also have a hopeful, creative and self-sacrificing side, thank God. We have the capacity, as individuals, to love. By that I mean not just passion but the sacrificial sort of love that balances sin—even original sin, the pride of thinking that we are God.[6]

G *(puzzled)*: I beg your pardon—you think of sin as the feeling that one is God? How queer. I'm afraid you must count me as one of the damned.

N: How so?

G: To my mind we *are* all God. We each share a portion of the Truth, which is to say, a portion of the divine.

N *(frowning)*: A pleasant sentiment. But you must agree that the tendency to be presumptuous and the urge to lord it over others are deep in human nature.[7] And inextricable from it.

G *(agreeing)*: Oh yes. Untruth is ubiquitous, I'm afraid. But as you say, fortunately humans have a capacity for being creative and self-sacrificing. To achieve freedom we have to make a voluntary act of continuous self-sacrifice.[8] [Smiling optimistically] If an army wages war against us, how fortunate that we can appeal to that higher level in our nature. Only it can dispel the rude force of might.

N *(disapprovingly):* Not quite so fast. I'm not even sure that works very well for you and me. I'm far less convinced that moral suasion has any real power where groups are concerned. Certainly not armies!

G: How so?

N: Well my dear Mr. Gandhi, it seems to me that groups have less reason to guide and check impulse, less capacity for self-transcendence, less ability to comprehend the needs of others than do the individuals who compose them. Personal relationships, thank goodness, are a cut above.[9]

G: Indeed? Are groups so ethically bankrupt? How do you account for that?

N: Egoism. Collective pride. Every individual has such tendencies too, but they achieve a more vivid expression and a more cumulative effect when they are united in a common impulse.[10]

G *(concluding for him):* . . . so groups are always morally inferior to individuals?

N *(triumphantly):* Exactly.

G: Well how gloomy we are, Mr. Niebuhr.

N: No, just realistic. I prefer to be thought of as realistic.

G: And the rest of us are unrealistic, I suppose.

N: With all due respect, you do have a bit of difficulty in comprehending the modern world. You regard it all as some sort of Indian family.

G: And?

N: And it's not. A tangle of organizational networks, that's what it is. Entities that possess no locus of accountability or authority; social behemoths that lumber mindlessly, amorally along.[11]

G: Dreadful thing, modern society. I agree. But my dear Mr. Niebuhr, you should peer through the glass walls. There are people inside. They have minds and morals, and even a bit of your precious love.

N: But not on company time. [He looks at Gandhi carefully.] You know, you have a lot in common with Karl Marx.

G (taken aback): Good gracious. What a comparison!

N: Indeed. Both of you have an astute political sense, but muddled with morality. Both of you have a somewhat sentimental view of human nature—Marx with his quixotic hopes for revolution, and you with your touching reliance on passive resistance.[12] As if good will could bring about political change!

G: Please. Not "passive resistance." Call it "soul force" or "truth force" or something else. There's nothing passive about it.[13] And as for political change—well, I suppose modesty should prevent me from saying anything about our gaining India's national freedom. After all . . .

N (interrupting): Aha! Force!

G (startled): I beg your pardon?

N: You said "force."

G: Well yes, of course.

N: That's the whole point. You've admitted that you are yourself much too realistic a politician to be a pacifist. You could never commit yourself to a real nonresistance, now could you?[14]

G (agreeably): Quite right. I never claimed to do so.

N: But you claim nonviolence . . .

G: Adamantly.

N: A nonviolence that is force?

G: Truth force, yes.

N (pressing the point): Well then. Your nonviolence may in fact coerce and destroy.[15]

G (trying to understand): You mean if it is, well . . . pushy.

N: Pushy, precisely. When nonviolent resistance places physical restraints on the desires and activities of others, it is a form of coercion, my friend.[16]

G (eager to defend his position): Yes, but you see . . .

N (interrupting with a magnanimous wave of his hand): No, no. No need to apologize. I quite understand. You needn't be embarrassed about having to use a little coercion now and then.

We all have to do it. No good would come in the world otherwise.

G *(trying to interrupt):* Well, but . . .

N *(pressing on):* Not that I find using it a cheery prospect. All
coercion—physical, psychic—is dangerous. Its ultimate value
depends on the social purpose for which it is enlisted.[17] But if
there is a noble end in view, the means to be chosen is really a
matter more political than it is ethical.[18]

G *(forcibly):* False!

N *(surprised):* Beg pardon? Perhaps you didn't hear. I said . . .

G: I heard perfectly well. You said the means are justified by a
decent end. And I said, false!

N: Mine is a perfectly moral position.

G: Except that it is simply untrue. If you fight with violence and
deceit, you'll come to a violent and deceitful conclusion, no
matter how fine your original goal.

N: Well now, my dear Mr. Gandhi, you yourself scarcely a minute
ago admitted to the use of coercion in your own campaigns.

G *(raising his voice slightly):* I did nothing of the sort. That was
your conclusion, to which you rushed so eagerly, preventing me
from any response of my own.

N *(graciously):* Well then . . .

G: Well what?

N: Respond.

G: You see I wanted to make a distinction between coercive nonviolence and noncoercive nonviolence.

N: I think you have it a bit confused. The distinction you want to
make is between active and passive nonviolence. You have
adopted the virtue of the latter while applying the force of the
former.[19]

G: No, that's your distinction, not mine. The point is not whether
nonviolence is active or passive—although the active kind is
likely to be more effective—but whether it's coercive. The coercive kind is simply a pressure tactic that replaces physical weapons with psychological and emotional manipulation.[20]

N *(agreeably):* Precisely. My point all along, and it is the reason why I think your insistence on nonviolence is so misleading. There is scarcely a line at all between violent and nonviolent coercion. We have no disagreement there!

G: Quite so. But my dear friend, my form of nonviolence is not coercion at all. Mine is *noncoercive* nonviolence, and it is quite different.

N *(skeptically):* Different? Indeed?

G: Mine is the ardent attempt to resolve disputes amicably by shifting to a broad position that incorporates both of the adversaries' points of view.

N *(somewhat impatient):* Oh that. Your moral suasion. I regard it as a sort of ethical education.[21] It's all quite fine and I'm certainly in favor of more of it, but you see that's just the sort of thing that collectivities are not capable of, even if individuals, at least the more civil ones, are. I told you that at the outset.

G: But did you hear me agree?

N: Look around you. Organizations are governed solely by self-interest.

G: And yet the courageous voice makes all the difference. Look at your Martin Luther King, Jr.

N *(brightening):* A fine fellow, yes. And effective. You must be pleased that he read so many of your works at an early age.

G *(brushing off the compliment):* And yours as well, I understand. But did I hear you say that he was effective? And was he not also—I hesitate to remind you—nonviolent?

N: Yes, but coercively nonviolent. As you yourself were. And properly so. For minorities and those in positions of military weakness, nonviolent tactics can be the most effective—perhaps the *only* effective—means of achieving just goals. Why I myself recommended in 1932 that the American Negroes adopt such a strategy, and that was 30 years before the civil rights movement.[22]

G *(shaking his head):* Oh my brother. We come so close to agreement and then . . . You see, my point of view is just the opposite. I think nonviolence is effective only for the strong, never for the weak.[23] And in my view it was King and his followers' organizational and moral strength that gave them power. With this, they could fight noncoercively, engage the moral conscience of the nation and move it to change. Your pushy strategies would have only led to a backlash of resentment from the privileged ones.

N   *(softly):* And I see these things so fraught with ambiguity: coercion and noncoercion, love and force, self-interest and self-sacrifice. They are yoked together. One always lurks behind the other.

G   *(surprised at this shift in tone):* Love and force? Then you can imagine a social force that is propelled by love?

N   *(almost wistfully):* Oh yes, my yes, although never solely by love. Yet I can't imagine a greater contribution we could make than to bring the force of love to political life. To recognize that the evil in the foe is always in the self, and to lay claim to the impulses of love that tie all people together in spite of social conflict—these are the peculiar gifts of religion to the human spirit. Secular imagination is not capable of producing them, for they require a sublime madness which disregards immediate appearances and emphasizes profound and ultimate unities.[24] And if in a social conflict, justice is achieved, but the spiritual element of nonviolence is lost, something essential to the social character will be lost as well.[25]

ꙮ Issue #4:
Was Gandhi Always a Gandhian?
—MOHANDAS *v.* THE MAHATMA

Until now we have been largely concerned with the Gandhi of ideas rather than the Gandhi of action. The focus has been on his method of peaceful fighting, and the other issues in his life—his personal, social, and political concerns—have been set aside. Yet it should be clear by now that Gandhian logic insists that ideas and action should be seen as interconnected.

In fact, although the Gandhian approach to conflict can be used as simply a technique, the extent of its potential is far greater than that. And, if you accept the idea that the means are as important as the goal, and that the ultimate conflict—the struggle against untruth —never really ends, you are pushed in the direction of understanding the Gandhian method as more than just an occasional tactic. You may see it instead as a continuing pattern of behavior—a way of life—and you are then faced with the question of whether you want to make it your own.

To find out what this means, you might turn to the accounts of the lives of those who have tried to live in an exemplary Gandhian fashion. These include Vinobe Bhave, Jayaprakash Narayan, and Mother Theresa in India; Danilo Dolci in Sicily; Chief Albert Luthuli in South Africa; and Dorothy Day, Thomas Merton, and Martin Luther King, Jr., in the United States.

But what better life to learn from than the life of Gandhi himself? Gandhi's actions spoke as eloquently as his words. For that reason, however, you may wonder whether they always communicated the same message. Was Gandhi's life a guide to his ideals?

In Gandhi's major campaigns the answer is, for the most part, yes. In fact he was often more consistent in conducting these actions than he was in expounding his thoughts, and scholars such as Joan Bondurant have gained a great deal of insight into the Gandhian method by analyzing the structure of these campaigns.

But in other instances there were divergences between what he said and what he did, and it is these that we will explore here. Some of the differences between the real and the ideal Gandhi are easy enough to ignore. They involved brief moments of obstinacy and pretension—weaknesses that plague us all—and can be readily excused. But other strains were more significant, tendencies in his behavior that seemed to contradict the most fundamental ideals of *satyagraha:* noncoercion, openness to change, and a willingness to consider alternative interpretations of the truth.

When such basic matters are at issue, Gandhian theory advises a confrontation, so that truth can win out. And no one is in a better position to do the fighting about Gandhi than Gandhi himself. In this chapter then, Mahatma Gandhi—the Gandhi of ideas—challenges Mohandas Gandhi, the Gandhi of actions. But before the two have at it, it would be well to review the major contours of the life they shared. This will set the context for the incidents about which Mohandas and the Mahatma will debate.

Gandhi did not start life a *mahatma*, a "great soul." He began it, in 1869, as Mohandas Karamchand Gandhi. It was an inquisitive but not extraordinary lad who grew up in the town of Porbandar, northwest of Bombay, and was involved in the usual mischief to which youths are susceptible. Young Mohandas came to his moral positions over time, through testing and mistakes—"experiments with truth," as he called them.[1]

Like most Indians Gandhi married early, and his wife, Kasturbai, came to play a strong supportive role throughout his life. In 1888 Gandhi embarked for London to study law, expecting to return and assume his father's duties as prime minister of a princely state. In London he aspired to look and act "like an English gentleman," as he put it, and became involved in a somewhat odd circle of social-ists, pacifists, theosophists, and freethinkers at the vegetarian restau-rant where he had his fare.[2]

Returning to India, he found that the family's traditional adminis-trative role was no longer secure and no position stood waiting. Within a year he set sail again, this time bound for South Africa. There he set up a law practice in Durban, and soon became in-volved in a struggle to protect the rights of the expatriate Indian community.

Gandhi's involvement began in response to personal insults: he was not allowed to wear his turban in the courtroom and he was tossed off a train for insisting on traveling first class with the whites. He saw himself as a victim of the "deep disease of color prejudice,"[3] and his own obstinate refusal to yield to racial injustice soon became the focus for many others' resistance as well. It was the beginning of *satyagraha*.

Gandhi returned to India in 1915, at the age of 46. He had scarcely visited his homeland since he was a child, but his reputation as the leader of an effective movement against British rule in South Africa had traveled ahead of him, and within three years he had made his way into the inner circle of India's embryonic nationalist movement. As his fame spread to the countryside, Gandhi's political reputation took on a spiritual glow, and his name became embel-lished with honorifics: Gandhi became Gandhiji; Mohandas became Mahatma.

He established an ashram, a sort of political commune, near the city of Ahmedabad, and named it *satyagraha*, to convey "both our goal and our method of service."[4] Gandhi's first *satyagraha* cam-paigns in India were waged over economic issues—disputes involv-ing plantation and factory workers—and then the struggles became focused on the central issue of the day, India's desire to be indepen-dent from the British.

Gandhi became caught up in a maelstrom of political activity. Between 1919 when he organized a national strike against the Rowlatt Bills—a British attempt to stifle nationalist activities—and 1930 when he led a massive march to the sea, Gandhi conducted a series of major campaigns against the colonial government. He claimed that these campaigns were not only assaults on British rule but also conscious attempts to experiment in nonviolent methods. Although some of the most creative of Gandhi's endeavors at social change on a local level were yet to come, these were the most important years in the development of *satyagraha* as a mass movement.

Gandhi's activities culminated in his return to London in 1931, where he was a central figure in the Round Table Conference. The meeting, which brought together high British officials and representatives of the Indian nationalist movement, was held for the purpose of negotiating a greater degree of home rule for Indians. Its results were regarded at the time as something of a triumph for the nationalists. But one outcome was unexpected, and for Gandhi, unwelcome: the British-proposed plan to allot separate legislative seats for Untouchables. Gandhi thought it was an attempt to sever the "indivisible family" of Hindu society,[5] and in 1932 undertook a fast against it. In the end a compromise ensued, which allowed for certain seats to be reserved exclusively for Untouchable candidates but mandated that they be elected by the general populace.

After his "epic fast," as he proclaimed it, Gandhi virtually disappeared from politics, claiming that he had been converted to the cause of social change from within as a prerequisite to India's freedom from forces outside.[6] He may have sensed, in part, that his massive protest campaigns were no longer as appropriate as they once had been. Other nationalist leaders had turned their attention to electoral challenges and the politics of negotiation. So Gandhi withdrew, devoting himself to village economic schemes, to his writings, and to an attempt to create a Gandhian form of education.

Only when the political climate had radically changed did Gandhi emerge from retirement. In 1942 he stepped into the limelight once again to join a new nationalist effort, a massive movement of noncooperation against the British, who were now mired in the exigencies of war. The British nipped any new aspirations for independence in the bud by arresting the nationalists, including Gandhi, and letting them sit out most of the rest of the war years in jail.

By 1946, however, the British were exhausted. Depleted by the war and battered by unending nationalist struggles, they finally capitulated to the demand that India be free. Yet the new India was to stand divided, with a separate nation—Pakistan—carved out of the subcontinent for Muslims. Gandhi was deeply disappointed that an independent India should be born in fragments, and refused to take part in the ceremonies marking India's liberation on August 15, 1947. He refused even to give an interview to the BBC.[7]

Instead he threw himself into a series of futile attempts to stop the bloody riots that attended the partitioning of the subcontinent as Hindus and Sikhs were uprooted from their homes and livelihoods in Pakistan, and Muslims fled the new India. Gandhi undertook another fast, this time for the sake of Hindu-Muslim unity, and won a pledge from leaders of some of the more militant religious groups to cease their violence.

The pledge was not terribly effective, and it was a member of one of the radical Hindu groups who fired the gun that killed the Mahatma as he was on his way to afternoon prayers in Delhi on January 30, 1948. Gandhi died with a name for God, *Ram*, on his lips, in the midst of a campaign against what he regarded as untruth. It is perhaps fitting that his struggle was incomplete—his *satyagraha*, as so often happens, unfulfilled.

That evening, India's new Prime Minister, Jawaharlal Nehru, announced on national radio that "the light has gone out." But he went on to say that this was only true in a very limited sense, "for the light that shone in this country was no ordinary light."[8] These words only confirmed what many had long believed—that the man was a saint.

Gandhi continues to be remembered as a luminary—an extraordinary, even holy, man. Saintliness indeed may have been something to which he himself aspired. Yet because his history is so recent, the humble, sometimes imperfect details of his life still protrude through the myths. This allows us to see him as a person like ourselves in some ways, a person whose real and ideal selves differed and at times warred with each other.

In what follows, then, the ideal, theoretical Gandhi—Gandhiji, the Mahatma—is pitted against his historical half-brother, Mohandas. No doubt they argued with one another frequently during Gandhi's lifetime. Here the debate is continued through a series of imaginary letters; a troubled, occasionally pointed exchange.

October 18, 1901

Dear Mohandas:

It has come to my attention that you have forced your wife to return some gifts that she received as going-away presents when you and she left Durban—some jewelry and the like. Apparently you and she had quite a verbal brawl; my sympathies.

However much I may concur with your general sentiment in the matter—that a public worker should, as a matter of principle, accept no costly gifts[9]—something disturbs me about this incident. I think it has to do with the way you have made Kasturbai comply.

As I recall, Kasturbai claimed not to want the ornaments for herself but for her future daughters-in-law, and as a sort of financial protection—for you certainly have done little for your family in that regard. Besides, she said that the ornaments had been meant for her, not for you, and that considering all that she had done for you—she claimed to have "toiled and moiled for you day and night"—she deserved them.[10]

You admitted that these were pointed thrusts, and that some of them struck home.[11] Yet you refused to budge, and the trinkets were returned to the giver, who sold them and put the profits into a trust fund on which you later were able to draw for public purposes.[12] From your wife's point of view, this must have appeared as little more than a clever way of appropriating her jewelry for your own purposes.

By the way, do you really think it wise to let people call you Mahatma? It seems a bit, well, vaunted. Try reducing yourself to a zero.[13]

Yours,
Gandhi

Dear Gandhiji:

I am flattered by the concern you have shown in your letter. But also a bit puzzled.

Regarding those annoying gifts: surely you would not have allowed me to keep them! The money they brought, after all, was used for very good purposes.

And what sort of example would I have set for my wife and children, whom I am trying to train for a life of service?[14] Kasturbai is such a simple woman, not at all educated, and I have had to teach her everything, make her learn what I have learned.[15] Truly, I have had to serve as her moral guide.

Perhaps you wish people did not have to play such a role for others, but sometimes it is simply necessary. It is not so odd, after all, in our culture.

Having a family has not always been an easy thing for me. Early in my youth I learned that if I were to embrace the whole world I should have to avoid exclusive intimacies.[16] Family relationships, therefore, have always been something of a bother. I would like to regard all of India as my family instead.[17]

I do hope that you will understand, and forgive my moral impatience.

Respectfully,
Mohan (not Mahatma)

Dear Mohandas:

Whether you intended to gain from putting the gifts in trust is neither here nor there. Rather, I think the issue is Kasturbai, and whether you really honored her point of view.

If her points struck home, as you have said, wasn't it necessary to incorporate them into the solution? You latched onto one principle and clung to it in your disagreement with her, but it was not the only principle involved. Some recognition of Kasturbai's contributions was also called for, and some show of responsibility for your family.

I'm concerned about two things here, and they are linked to each other. One is the way you rushed to conclusions about what was truthful before taking Kasturbai's perspective into account, forgetting that what is truth for one person may be untruth for another.[18] The other is the way you bludgeoned her into submission with your heavy-handed insistence on public morality. The golden rule of conduct, after all, is mutual toleration.[19]

Yours,
Gandhi

Dear Gandhiji:

Just a note to thank you for your response. Don't you think it is necessary, however, to impress on others the importance of virtue?[20]

Respectfully,
Mohan

Dear Mohandas:

Thanks for the note. I hate to harp on the point, but it seems to me that much of the luster of virtue is lost when you push it on others. The imposition of your notion of truth on others is an insufferable interference with their freedom of conscience.[21] Those closest to you are frequently the greatest victims of this—especially your own family.

This is not the first time this has happened. I remember that dreadful incident several years ago in Durban when Kasturbai drew the line at cleaning out the chamber pot of an Indian guest of Untouchable ancestry, even though you had done that sort of thing yourself.[22] She told you to keep house for yourself, and you actually dragged her to the gate before she told you to stop making a fool of yourself, and you came to your senses. It was a simple household quarrel, to be sure, but it indicates how your fearsome insistence on your own way in moral matters can brutalize those around you.

Take your children—what a peculiar and strict upbringing you gave them, even depriving them of a decent schooling. It's not their fault you hold modern education in contempt. No wonder Harilal rebelled, and lived, from your point of view, a life of profligacy. His goal, apparently, was to become rich, and easily at that.[23] His was scarcely a laudable goal, I agree, but look at what it signified. It appears that he wanted desperately to assert himself, and felt you had denied him that right.

I wouldn't want you to ignore issues affecting the morality of others, especially those in your own family. But it is wrong to force your view on them. That denies their own integrity; it violates their individuality. We must measure people with their own measure and see how far they come up to it.[24]

Yours,
Gandhi

＊　　＊　　＊　　＊

July 1, 1914

Dear Mohandas:

I see you have been at it again. Only now it's a political issue instead of a personal one.

Your victory over General Smuts in South Africa has been widely praised as an example of how one should defend the rights of people of color in that nation—an important principle, indeed. My only question is whether it was the principle that triumphed, or you.

Smuts was hampered and hurt by your nonviolent campaigns, I'm afraid. He recalled the whole thing as a "trying situation," and as everyone knows, he eventually capitulated.[25] But capitulated to what? He admired you as a tactician, but there is no indication that he was ever won over to your view on the principle for which you fought. Should you ever leave South Africa, the conditions of Indians and Blacks are liable to become as oppressive as they were before.[26]

Yours,
Gandhi

Dear Gandhiji:

It is a chilling prediction that you have made, especially since I am indeed about to leave. I will keep it in mind and continue to maintain interest in the South African situation on my return to the homeland.[27]

I accept your view that the process of *satyagraha* is an ongoing one, and that what seems a clear victory at the time may in hindsight seem like only a minor skirmish in a protracted war.

Respectfully,
Mohan

Dear Mohandas:

I'm afraid you may have missed the point. It is true that you have sometimes proclaimed a victory prematurely, but that was not what really troubled me.

My concern was that Smuts seemed entirely unconverted to your principle. Your nonviolence forced him to accede, but that is not *satyagraha*. Our motto must always be conversion by gentle persuasion.[28]

You have been so intent on getting a principle across that at times you have become more coercive than persuasive. You have done so nonviolently, of course, but that is not the issue. What seems to be *satyagraha* can sometimes be its opposite: *duragraha,* the force of coercion.[29] To practice true *satyagraha* is not to disavow just physical violence, but mental violence as well. It is not right to assume that real *satyagraha* has occurred when all one knows is that a bloodless form of manipulation has succeeded.

Yours,
Gandhi

*   *   *   *

JUNE 22 1918 KHEDA
JUST RECEIVED WORD THAT YOU ARE SUPPORTING BRIT-

ISH WAR EFFORT STOP EVEN RECRUITING SOLDIERS STOP
HAVE YOU ABANDONED YOUR MIND STOP

SIGNED GANDHI

June 24, 1918

Dear Gandhiji,

I have received your telegram with sadness. It seems that no one is much in favor of this. Everyone thinks I am just deluding myself.[30] Even the villagers heckle me.

At the time it seemed a good idea to raise a large Indian contingent to support the British war effort. I thought maybe it would bring us respect, and cause the British to treat us like partners in the Empire.[31] Besides, we need to learn the use of weapons for self-defense. There are times when such weapons are required, as when one must kill a dog with rabies[32] or halt an invading foreign army.[33]

A time of war poses great problems for someone pledged to nonviolence. If one's country is fighting, there is no way to escape from the war effort. No choice is a good one.

In the Boer War, and earlier on in this one, I organized an ambulance corps—an acceptable alternative to combat, I'm sure you will agree. I've always respected the good things about British civilization and felt they were worth fighting for. And it is not so odd for me to respect the military, now is it? Think of its discipline and bravery, its resolve.[34]

True nonviolence involves a paradox: we must have the strength to kill before we have the ability to transcend killing.[35] A weak and effeminate nation cannot perform this grand act of renunciation.[36] So although I am recruiting soldiers for war, I am also recruiting for principles: the value of British civilization, and the strength necessary for nonviolence. These principles are worthy of support, I believe, and I hope you will feel the same.

Faithfully yours,
Mohandas

JUNE 27 1918
SUPPORT THE PRINCIPLES STOP NOT THE WAR STOP
                                                    SIGNED GANDHI

*   *   *   *

                                                    September 20, 1932
Dear Mohandas:

I understand that today you are planning to "enter the fiery gate," as you put it [37]—a fast unto death. This is a very serious matter. Do you really think the issue warrants such extreme behavior?

The principle, that of making certain that Untouchables are included in Hindu society, is an important one. But I have heard no one espouse the contrary view. Your opposition—the Untouchables themselves, at least those led by Dr. Ambedkar—also hopes for a better role for the outcastes.[38] It is true that some Untouchables regard Hinduism as oppressive, and want to disassociate themselves from it. But no one has suggested that they secede from the nation, which is what you appear to be struggling against.

Have you really waged a careful search for the truth in this matter? Perhaps you should talk again with Dr. Ambedkar.

                                                    Yours,
                                                    Gandhi

Dear Gandhiji:

With due respect, my real opposition is not Ambedkar but the prejudices of the upper castes. I understand why the Untouchable leaders distrust me, since I am a member of a superior class, as it is miscalled.[39]

But even though "touchable" by birth, I am an Untouchable by choice, and I think I qualify to represent them, even their lowest strata,[40] as well as Dr. Ambedkar does. I would, however, be delighted to talk with him and any other friends.[41] But let the fast continue.

Respectfully,
Mohandas

Dear Mohandas:

I'm not sure which disturbs me more, the coercive tone of your approach or your obstinacy in refusing to see Ambedkar's point of view. You seem to have missed my main point: fighting for the truth means fighting for the whole truth, not just your portion of it. Truth always comes in fragments, from different angles of vision.[42]

I know you are in the midst of a struggle, and I know that there are times when one simply has to go ahead and take a stand, and defend the right as much as it is humanly possible to see it.[43] But you cannot stay content with that. You must continue to be willing to revise your goals.

I suppose what upsets me most is your plan to carry on this fast "until the end."[44] Now really, how do you expect anyone to respond to that?

Fasting is the ultimate weapon, the most infallible device in the armory of *satyagraha*.[45] To fast is to take the extreme violence of a situation and turn it toward oneself in the attempt to vindicate the principle at issue. But such an act violates life—one's own life—and can be justified only in the most unusual situations, and only as a last resort.[46]

I can imagine sacrificing oneself, but only if it would help stop a terrible violence—if, for example, it would bring peace to a catastrophic war. Has the issue for which you are fasting the clarity and the severity to deserve such a response?

Yours,
Gandhi

Dear Gandhiji:

I don't know. I may be wholly wrong; that is quite possible.[47] But it's also quite irrelevant to the present purpose. So long as I am as right as is humanly possible, I must go on to the farthest end.[48]

But I can tell you this for certain. The principle underlying this fast—my opposition to the oppression of Untouchables—is worth staking the rest of my life on. Nothing will satisfy me until the last vestige of untouchability is gone.[49] Already I have dedicated myself to just this goal. I intend to retire from politics and return to rural life and simple values, and see what can be done to lighten the wretched burden of these people.

Perhaps I have misused *satyagraha*. The approach is in its infancy, after all, and therefore not yet perfected.[50] But I still regard it as a path worth taking not only for the resolution of political clashes but for overcoming the deep disharmonies of human existence. Ultimately the truth worth searching for is a transcendent truth, a pattern of love and reconciliation that knits together discordant lives, revolutionizes social ideals, and makes people, and the communities of which they are a part, whole.[51]

I don't pretend to have a grasp on all of this already. I am, after all, a mortal and a humble seeker.[52] My conviction that a truth such as this is actually obtainable is a conviction, nothing more. But I find it impossible to escape my trust that in the struggle of life one actually can conquer hate by love, untruth by truth, and violence by self-suffering.[53]

> Respectfully,
> Mohandas Gandhi

❧ The Issues That Remain

In this and the previous section of the book, Gandhi's ideas have been submitted to a rather harsh scrutiny. They have been tested in a variety of cases, some of his most difficult critics have attempted to take them apart, and the inconsistencies between his theories and some of his own actions have been examined. Despite all this, the Gandhian ideas have emerged intact, if not entirely unscathed. Still, some issues remain.

Arrogance and Double Advocacy

Among the remaining issues is the matter of truth and how it is determined. In the epic fast and in some of the domestic disputes with his wife, Gandhi showed a tendency to leap to his own conclusions about what was right, and to hold onto his views with an inflexibility that some might regard as self-righteous. It was a tendency of Gandhi's that troubled Freud—at least the Freud of the imaginary conversations with Gandhi—but Gandhi certainly was not the only person who has behaved with such self-assuredness. Some of the characters in the case studies were equally emphatic in their moral assertiveness, and in conflicts that you and I encounter every day the same tendency often prevails. It is difficult to bear the discomfort of uncertainty, so we easily fall into the assumption that our own ways of getting on with life must be right. Perhaps we should not be too hard on Gandhi for doing the same. But how can this rigidity be avoided?

One answer would be to apply the process of *double advocacy,* the idea that one should attempt to argue for the truth of both sides of a dispute.

This idea is based on several Gandhian concepts. One is the Gandhian refusal to identify the absolute truth with any existing moral code or religious tradition. The Gandhian approach reminds us that there are many versions of truth, and each side has only a partial view of the whole. Another idea of Gandhi's that is relevant here is the notion that truth is not something we can know before we act, but something we move towards in the process of acting. From this point of view, a true position cannot be discerned prior to an encounter; rather, it should emerge from it. Even the Gandhian rule of reverence for all life is not a statement of what is true, but a guide to being truthful, for the Gandhian concept of truth is not a principle but a process.

I believe that this conviction undergirded Gandhi's own approach to conflicts in his life. But the fact remains that most of his writings and actions were not about how to *find* the truth, but how to hold fast to it so that the truthful solution could win out. This obstinacy makes Gandhi appear at times to be morally arrogant, to deny his opponents' view a fair hearing.

Gandhi's stubborn attitude is not without its Gandhian justification, however. The Gandhian technique requires the fighter at some point in the struggle to "hold firm to the truth," as the term *satyagraha* implies.

But to which version of truth should you and I hold firm, and at what point in our struggles? If we latch onto a truthful solution too late, we may weaken our case. Yet if we move too soon, we may silence our opponents and keep them from speaking. Then at some later date we may find that our opponents had some claim to the truth all along.

The two requirements of openness and conviction may appear to be a contradiction in Gandhian thought. And perhaps some tension between them is inevitable. Yet I think it is possible to separate the two requirements and acknowledge both simultaneously. The fight for truth and the search for it can be waged at the same time, but separately. Rather than thinking of these two as sequential steps, I suggest we think of them as parallel or as alternating frequencies. This way it is clear that the search for a better solution ought to continue even while we hold firm to the truthful resolution that is at hand.

If both parties enter into the search for truth, this dual process can take place rather easily. But even if one side is unwilling, as so often happens, we can do something to maintain the simultaneity of conviction and search. We can conduct our opponents' participation in the search for truth by proxy, imagining their perspective and defending the truthful elements in it.

We then act as advocates for both our side and our opponents', arguing as vigorously and convincingly for the other side as for our own. And as a judge does with attorneys in chamber, we try to get the quarrelling positions in our mind to come to some sort of consensus—a tentative agreement that can be renegotiated as the struggle develops.

This process of double advocacy need exist only in our own imaginations. It need not intrude on the fight itself unless, of course, our silent deliberations result in a reformulation of the goal. In any case, that is not its major purpose. What double advocacy is intended to provide is a critical perspective on the whole process. It keeps us involved in *satyagraha* by preventing us from getting trapped in our own narrow vision of the truth. And it reassures us that even though what is right is not always immediately apparent in any given situation, the task of searching for a solution is itself an act of truth.

Detentive Coercion and Enabling Means

Another problem that surfaced in the case studies and the discussions is one that appears in the next phase of a conflict, when the opponents battle to have their view of a truthful resolution heard and accepted. Opponents need to be forceful in their efforts to do so, but this is where the difficulty arises. How can they be forceful without being coercive?

Gandhi claimed that his actions were never coercive. But since his opponents often regarded them as such, I am tempted to agree with the assertion of Reinhold Niebuhr that Gandhi sometimes sacrificed his noncoercive ideals for the sake of effectiveness.

There is a tension between force and love that is built into the very nature of *satyagraha*: a conflict between firmness (*agraha*) on the one hand and selfless nonviolence (an aspect of *satya*) on the other. This leads to an ambivalence towards force in Gandhian thought.

Gandhi argued that the two could easily go together, but in his own life the tension between force and love was sometimes striking. Gandhi's fascination with the military way of life, for example, seems hard to reconcile with his insistence on turning the other cheek, and his attempt to recruit soldiers for the British seems downright bizarre. The forcefulness with which he waged campaigns often bordered on coercion—Niebuhr said that he frequently stepped over the line—and never was this tendency so obvious and dangerous as when he engaged in fasting as a tactic of persuasion.

Much as Gandhi wanted nonviolence and force to be compatible with each other, there are times when it seems that Karl Marx was right: we are compelled to choose one or the other. Even Gandhi had to admit that this is sometimes so.

Suppose, for instance, that you are suddenly faced with a scene of brutal violence—rape was the example Gandhi chose. What should you do? Gandhi argued that a man "who allows the modesty of a woman to be outraged" when she is under attack by a rapist "will be regarded as a coward." Such a coward would be "a partner in violence" with the rapist, said Gandhi, who concluded that "heroic violence is less sinful than cowardly nonviolence."[1]

Similarly, a sniper taking aim might well be halted in midaction by the Gandhian, who would be justified in attempting to wrestle the gun away. Both the rapist and the sniper would in essence be saved from themselves, for violence would be destructive not only to the targets of such aggression but to the character of the aggressors as well.

Even in these rare cases where coercion is permitted, Gandhians are obliged to take into account the welfare of the opponent. They are constrained to think of that kind of force in the same way that they would think of any other tactic in a fight—as a brief moment in a larger process of reconciliation. The violence itself is never applauded, of course, but the interesting thing is that Gandhi could conceive of an instance in which the use of coercion is justified.

Another situation in which a Gandhian might have to resort to coercion—although Gandhi did not actually say so—is one in which the moral fighter lacks the strength to engage fully in *satyagraha*. Gandhi frequently argued that nonviolence was effective only for the strong, and his prescription for greater strength was perfectly clear: increase the size and resolve of the Gandhian group. But what if that is not possible? What if one faces circumstances such as those that the Jews in Warsaw encountered? Is it not possible that *satyagraha* can be initiated only through coercion in such dreadful cases?

The very mention of these possibilities may make you feel that we are slipping away from the core of Gandhi's approach, the thing that gave it such unusual strength all along. And yet we are faced with the fact that Gandhi envisioned some rare cases in which coercion, even physical assaults, were justified. How can this apparent contradiction in Gandhian thought be reconciled?

It may be well at this point to look at the kind of coercion Gandhi absolutely proscribed and distinguish it from the kind he occasionally justified. Perhaps the line can be drawn in a way that will maintain the core of the Gandhian rule of nonviolence, yet allow for times when an element of coercion is unavoidable.

This line is one that separates the sort of coercion that destroys from the sort that merely disables or detains for a period of time. The latter term—*detentive coercion*—applies to any force that you use to keep your opponent from doing something violent. This kind of coercion is usually brief and reversible. But destructive coercion —the attempt to damage or obliterate your opponent—is quite different. The harm this sort of action creates may be a long time in healing. It may even be permanent.

Let there be no mistake: both detentive and destructive forms of coercion are violent. If you were awakened by the sound of a prowler in the middle of the night, you might snare the intruder with an animal trap or simply shoot for the heart. Both would be violent acts, and in a moment of panic you might feel that the circumstances would justify either. But if, when you turned on the lights, you discovered that the prowler was in fact your 12-year-old son raiding the refrigerator for a piece of chocolate cake, the distinction between the two would become crucial.

It is unfortunate that Gandhi did not make a clear theoretical distinction between the different forms of coercion. He rightly refused to distinguish between physical and emotional violence, but it seems to me that there is a great difference between destructive and detentive coercion. Gandhi himself tacitly recognized this when he engaged in certain actions and not others, and defended some kinds of coercion while condemning others.

If Gandhi had made a clear distinction between the different forms of coercion, he would have been in the company of several Christian pacifists who were making just this point during Gandhi's most active years. Among them were Clarence Marsh Case and Kirby Page.[2] The notion of detentive coercion was implicitly suggested by Page when he justified the occasional use of restraint if it was "administered in love."[3] Although Gandhi was aware of some of Page's writings—he even reprinted and circulated one of his pamphlets[4]—there is no indication that he was ever aware of Page's discussions of detentive coercion or seriously considered it.

That is a pity, for it could have provided greater consistency in Gandhi's ethics: as it is, there appears to be a gap between his proscription of coercion and his use of it. Gandhi might have employed the notion of detentive coercion in explaining how his ideas would work in those administrative structures where authority depends on the use of coercion, such as government and large organizations. Gandhi allowed a role for the coercive arm of public authority—the military and the police—but surely his thought was to limit their acts of coercion to the detentive kind. And the technical knowledge existed in Gandhi's time, as it certainly does in our own, for developing weapons that stun and temporarily disable opponents rather than hurting and killing them. It seems surprising that Gandhi did not draw attention to such techniques.

Perhaps he did not want to encourage even the detentive form of coercion, for it too has dangers. It can be misused, it can deny people their freedom, and it can harm. Many governments, for example, use the tactic of preventive detention to weaken political opposition; they imprison their opponents before they can attempt to come to power. In such cases detention is used as a device to destroy.

Then when are these forms of coercion legitimate? Seldom. According to Gandhian theory, all coercion, including the detentive kind, violates the rule that the means should be consistent with the ends. Detention by itself is consistent only with a goal that involves constant control over other people, and that no Gandhian can condone. So in order to justify any form of detentive coercion, detention must be combined with more positive acts, and the ends-means rule must be modified.

This amendment to the ends-means rule might be phrased as follows. You should try to use the truthful goal as the means in a fight, and the truthful means as a way of finding a goal, but when neither is possible, an alternative means may be devised for the sole purpose of enabling you to enter into the fray. This logic, which justifies a special *enabling means,* is applicable in circumstances in which the violence or intractability of the opponent, or a lack of resources on your own side, appears to leave you no choice but to apply a certain amount of coercive pressure.

It is reserved for desperate circumstances, and it justifies only a few instances of coercion, which must meet the following conditions. a) The action must have the effect of stopping a violent act in progress. b) It must only disable or detain, and not destroy. c) It must reduce the level of violence rather than increase it. d) It must make possible the beginning of a normal Gandhian fight, in which the fighter can revert to the general Gandhian principle and adopt the ends as the means.

Some might think that by providing for the possibility of any coercion at all in a Gandhian fight, even the relatively mild detentive kind, Pandora's box will open and endless brutalities will emerge. But I think this is not the case. The limitations on when such action may be undertaken are severe, and the action is always kept in check through double advocacy. The Gandhian is required to be painfully aware of what is being violated in instances when, for whatever reasons, coercion is allowed.

Organizational Fights and Counterstructures

The optimal way of producing change in a Gandhian fight is not through coercion, of course, but through conversion. The problem is that this requires an opponent who is capable of being converted. It is easiest to imagine such an opponent as an individual—someone who is at least potentially thoughtful and forgiving, someone capable of making a wide range of choices. This is the sort of opponent that Ms. A, Mr. B, and even Mr. C were. And many fights involve just such opponents.

Many, however, do not. As we saw in the case studies concerning terrorism in Northern Ireland and Jewish resisters in Warsaw, the opponents in many modern conflicts are not persons in any real sense. They are organizations, social systems, or policies that have no single mind directing them and, as Reinhold Niebuhr reminds us, no heart to grant them a moral conscience. Organizations are created and sustained by people, of course, but such people's choices are limited by the roles they play within an organization, and their conception of what the organization is and what it can do is usually fixed and limited. In light of this, an approach to social conflict based on the hope of personal charity and flexibility seems doomed.

Has *satyagraha* run head-on into an organizational wall? Some would say yes, that Gandhi's approach may be fine for interpersonal relations, but it is unrealistic for social conflicts on a grander scale.

This is a reasonable conclusion, but let us examine the other side of the issue. Gandhians hold that all conflicts are fundamentally the same—that is, they all arise out of clashes between principles—and the scale or nature of the opponent is immaterial. Moreover, most of Gandhi's own *satyagraha* campaigns were waged against political entities, not persons. His opponents included industries, local governments, and most notably, the entire British Empire.

How did Gandhi approach such entities? In a personal way, at times. In many cases he singled out particular individuals—generals, viceroys, and industrial managers—as spokespersons for their organizations and targets of his campaigns. He often had tea with the British viceroy, Lord Irwin, for instance, and he stayed in the home of a mill owner in Ahmedabad at the very time he was engaged in a labor strike against him. These were persons who had a great influence over the direction of their organizations, and Gandhi attempted to turn this to his benefit by confronting them personally.

There were also many instances when Gandhi did not make personal contact with leaders of the opposition. In such cases Gandhi appealed to the consciences of the many persons who comprised the whole organization. When Gandhi fought the governments of British India and South Africa, the circle of persons to whom he appealed ultimately included the entire citizenry of the oppressing nations. For this reason Gandhi carefully cultivated friendships with members of the domestic and foreign press. *Satyagraha* in these circumstances was a kind of public education, an attempt to awaken the conscience of a people.

The most important aspect of the large Gandhian campaigns, however, was something innovative, symbolized by Gandhi's salt kilns and spinning wheels. Here Gandhi attempted to provide alternative forms of organization through the campaigns themselves. While fighting with the British, he was busy creating *counterstructures* to what the British had laid down. In a classic case of using the ends as the means, he established the economic and political structures he hoped would replace the ones the British had imposed on him and his nation. It did not turn out quite that way; India eventually followed a rather different economic and political course than that plotted by Gandhi. But the point is that at the time, Gandhi was fighting British rule with a nascent rule of his own devising.

To see that Gandhi was engaged in building counterstructures to British rule is a far cry from envisioning Gandhi as a lone figure locked in a quixotic battle against an enormous enemy. It also defies the popular view that Gandhi could only appeal to the good will of the leaders of the organization he opposed. While some of Gandhi's actions seem to give these portrayals credibility, they can be viewed in another way. One can see these interpersonal encounters as skirmishes in a long struggle in which an old order was to be replaced with a new one, one Gandhi imagined to be more vital and true.

This point of view has implications for the way in which Gandhians should wage a fight against any organization. They should regard the struggle as one between structure and counterstructure, between competing visions of what kind of entity an organization should be and what path it should follow. The Gandhian side has the responsibility, then, of not only fighting against those policies that it doesn't like, but of attempting to bring about a structural change in the way in which the organization makes those policies.

As a result, the Gandhian approach to struggles with large entities must be somewhat different from what it is with individuals. The basic theory of conflict remains, but the emphasis is different. In personal quarrels, Gandhians devote much energy to improving the quality of the relationship between the Gandhian and the opponent. In large social struggles Gandhians aim for a change in the structures that govern relationships—the organizational communities in which people live and work.

For this reason a Gandhian fight with an organization often may not even look like a fight. The battle may involve a patient, long-range strategy for changing the system from within. Tactics may include attempts to democratize the selection of members of a governing board and attempts to institute new procedures for making decisions and formulating an organization's goals. Such a fight may involve very little confrontation. It may proceed instead through a series of behind-the-scenes attempts to challenge the established order with a carefully formulated plan for a more harmonious new one.

The Things That Endure

Because Gandhi's ideas sometimes were inconsistent with his own actions, and because there are gaps in Gandhian theory, we have had to fight a bit with him. But I trust the conflict has not been destructive. The ideas of double advocacy, detentive coercion, enabling means, and counterstructures are meant to add to Gandhi's strength, not diminish it.

Not that all the difficulties have been resolved. Many of you, no doubt, will still bridle at what Gandhi's critics have long seen as a utopian strain in his notion of society, a perfectionism in his view of human nature, and an only thinly disguised desire for power in his political actions. If you agree with Gandhi's critics, and find these characteristics objectionable, you may want to alter Gandhi's approach further—perhaps change it substantially—before you are ready to appropriate it.

Even so, I hope you will agree that there is much wisdom to be found in what Gandhi thought and did. The things that so passionately concerned and motivated him are worth taking seriously. If you wish to conduct your conflicts with the same degree of morality you find possible in quieter moments, if you want to encounter others with both force and love, if you are struggling to forge a link between private principles and public justice, and if you are trying to bridge the gap between your sense of ethics and what your professional roles require, then you have an ally in Gandhi. Allies should not be lightly dismissed.

Of course, this does not mean that you must accept Gandhi without reservation. You can fight with him, and you can stage your own experiments with truth. But if truth is your goal, or even if you simply harbor the hope of making your way through life's conflicts with a modicum of dignity and grace, then you may wish to try the Gandhian way—not just because of its esthetic appeal but because it works. It holds out the prospect of being able to fight yet at the same time be moral, to settle conflicts at their most basic levels, and to find resolutions in which both sides emerge as victors.

Finally, it introduces you to a kind of fighting that is its own reward. Even if nothing else is changed by waging your battles this way, you may be. And that is no mean gain.

Notes

Preface

1. *Young India,* August 11, 1920.

SECTION I: THE GANDHIAN FIGHT

My main sources of information about Gandhian ideas are the short essays of Gandhi's published in the journals *Indian Opinion, Young India,* and *Harijan.* Other references that follow are to collections of these essays under the titles *Ethical Religion* (1922; reprint, Madras, India: Ganesan Press, 1930), *Hind Swaraj or Indian Home Rule* (1909; reprint, Ahmedabad, India: Navajivan Publishing House, 1938), *From Yeravda Mandir* (1932; reprint, Ahmedabad, India: Navajivan Publishing House, 3rd ed., 1945), and *An Autobiography: The Story of My Experiments with Truth* (1927; reprint, Boston: Beacon Press, 1957), and also to *The Collected Works of Mahatma Gandhi* (New Delhi: Publications Division, Ministry of Information and Broadcasting, Government of India, 1958 to the present).

Chapter 1: Fighting a Gandhian Fight

1. *Young India,* November 5, 1919.
2. *Young India,* November 5, 1919.
3. *Young India,* September 23, 1926.
4. *Young India,* November 5, 1919.

Chapter 2: Why Fight at All?

1. *Harijan,* April 7, 1946.
2. *Young India,* October 31, 1929.
3. *Harijan,* October 3, 1936.
4. *Young India,* November 12, 1925.
5. *Harijan,* October 13, 1940.

Chapter 3: How Do You Know When You're Right?

1. *Yeravda Mandir,* 3.
2. *Yeravda Mandir,* 1.
3. *Yeravda Mandir,* 2.
4. This is the subtitle given the *Autobiography.*
5. *Harijan,* August 9, 1942.
6. *Ethical Religion,* 35.
7. *Young India,* March 9, 1922.
8. *Young India,* August 25, 1920.
9. *Young India,* November 5, 1919.
10. *Young India,* November 5, 1919.

Chapter 4: Violence: The Breakdown of a Fight

1. *Young India*, August 16, 1928.
2. *Yeravda Mandir*, 7.
3. *Yeravda Mandir*, 7.
4. *Young India*, August 25, 1920.
5. *Ethical Religion*, 43.
6. *Young India*, February 9, 1921.
7. *Hind Swaraj*, 59.
8. *Young India*, February 9, 1921.

Chapter 5: What to Do with a Recalcitrant Opponent

1. *Young India*, May 7, 1931.
2. *Young India*, May 7, 1931.
3. *Young India*, September 29, 1921.
4. *Young India*, May 7, 1931.
5. *Ethical Religion*, 43.

Chapter 6: The Weapon: The Goal Itself

1. *Yeravda Mandir*, 9.
2. *Collected Works*, 43:4.
3. *Young India*, June 25, 1925.
4. *Young India*, July 17, 1924.
5. *Young India*, December 18, 1924.
6. *Young India*, July 17, 1924.
7. *Young India*, December 18, 1924.

Chapter 7: The Power of Noncooperation

1. *Harijan*, March 10, 1946.
2. *Harijan*, March 10, 1946.
3. *Young India*, November 5, 1919.
4. *Young India*, October 25, 1921.
5. The phrase belongs to Richard B. Gregg, *The Power of Nonviolence* (New York: Schocken Books, 1966), passim.
6. *Young India*, August 12, 1926.
7. *Harijan*, March 20, 1937; April 2, 1938; October 14, 1939; October 21, 1939; March 17, 1946; *Young India*, December 31, 1931.
8. *Young India*, December 8, 1920.

Chapter 8: Fighting a Very Big Fight

1. *Young India*, August 11, 1920.
2. *Autobiography*, 325.
3. *Harijan*, March 6, 1939.
4. *Harijan*, March 6, 1939.
5. *Harijan*, June 10, 1939.
6. *Indian Opinion*, March 18, 1914.
7. *Collected Works*, 51:65.
8. This is the title of an essay in William James, *Memories and Studies* (New York: Longmans and Green, 1911).
9. *Young India*, September 22, 1920.
10. *Young India*, November 5, 1919.

11. Joan Bondurant, *Conquest of Violence*, (Princeton, N.J.:Princeton University Press, 1958; reprint, Berkeley and Los Angeles: University of California Press, 1967), 40-41.
12. *Harijan*, February 11, 1933.
13. *Harijan*, May 6, 1933.
14. *Harijan*, February 17, 1946.

Chapter 9: How Do You Know When You've Won?

1. *Harijan*, February 17, 1946.
2. Bondurant, *Conquest of Violence*, 67.
3. *Harijan*, February 17, 1946.
4. *Young India*, February 9, 1921.
5. *Young India*, January 26, 1922.
6. *Harijan*, April 7, 1946.
7. *Young India*, February 27, 1930.
8. *Young India*, January 21, 1920.
9. *Autobiography*, 366.

SECTION II: CASE STUDIES

Case #1: A Family Feud

This and the following two cases are fictionalized accounts based on actual incidents described in reports given by students in my graduate seminar in comparative ethics. The names and certain of the facts in the cases have been changed to protect the privacy of the participants.

1. *Autobiography*, 325.
2. *Ethical Religion*, 43.
3. *Harijan*, April 7, 1946.

Case #3: A Lonely Decision

1. *The Book of Discipline of the United Methodist Church* (Nashville: The United Methodist Publishing House, 1980), 90 and 184.
2. *The Book of Discipline*, 183.
3. *Ethical Religion*, 32.

Case #4: A Peaceful End to Irish Terrorism

In preparing this chapter I appreciated the comments and insight of two leaders in Northern Ireland, Lord Alderdice and David Trimble, who were kind enough to discuss the case with me. Both played significant roles in the Good Friday Agreement, for which Trimble received a Nobel Prize for Peace. Another first-person perspective on the making of the Good Friday Agreement may be found in George Mitchell, *Making Peace*. An overview of the history of Northern Ireland's troubles is provided in Michael Hughes, *Ireland Divided: The Roots of the Modern Irish Problem* and David McKittrick and David McVea, *Making Sense of the Troubles*, among many other such works available. For a discussion of the various options in attempting to resolve a violent conflict, especially ones involving terrorism, see the last chapter in my book, *Terror in the Mind of God: The Global Rise of Religious Violence*.

Case #5: A Tragic Resistance

Gandhi's position on the rise of the Nazi threat and the dilemma of the European Jews is found in his "Letter to Herr Hitler," his "Letter to Every Briton," and other letters and essays that have been collected in Ronald Duncan, ed., *Gandhi: Selected Writings*, pt. 3 (New York: Harper and Row, 1971) and the Navajivan Publishing House's *Selected Works of Mahatma Gandhi*, vol. 5 (Ahmedabad, India: 1968). For sources on the Jewish response to Gandhi I have been aided by Howard Simon, "In Pursuit of the Kingdom: A Study in the Ethics of Nonviolence in Gandhian and Traditional Jewish Thought" (B.A. honors thesis, Religious Studies Program, University of California, Berkeley, 1981). For information on the Warsaw ghetto uprising I have relied on Lucy S. Dawidowicz, *The War Against the Jews, 1933-1945* (New York: Holt, Rinehart and Winston, 1975).

1. For example, Bruno Bauer's book, *Die Judenfrage* (The Jewish Question), published in 1843, which prompted a response from Marx.
2. *Harijan*, November 26, 1938.
3. *Harijan*, November 26, 1938.
4. Reprinted in the *Inner Eye*, 219.
5. Martin Buber, "A Letter to Gandhi," in Buber and J. L. Magnes, *Two Letters to Gandhi* (Pamphlets of the Group "The Bond," Jerusalem: Rubin Mass, 1939), reprinted in Buber, *Pointing the Way*, (New York: Harper and Brothers, 1957):141.
6. *Harijan*, May 27, 1939.
7. *The War Against the Jews*, 301.
8. *The War Against the Jews*, 306.
9. *Young India*, August 12, 1926.
10. *Collected Works*, 51:80.
11. *Harijan*, March 20, 1937.
12. See Eberhard Bethge, *Bonhoeffer, Exile and Martyr* (London: Collins, 1975).

SECTION III: SOME SMALL QUARRELS

Issue #1: Can Violence Ever Be Justified? *(Marx v. Gandhi)*

My main source of information on Marx's thought is his own writing, the most complete collection of which is found in *Karl Marx, Frederick Engels: Collected Works* (hereafter *Collected Works*), published in English translation in Moscow in 1978 and issued in the United States through International Publishers, New York. Briefer collections of Marx's writings that I have found useful are the early humanistic works translated and published by the Foreign Languages Publishing House, Moscow, including the collection *Marx and Engels on Religion*, republished in America by Schocken Books, New York, in 1964 with an introduction by Reinhold Niebuhr, and reissued by Scholars Press, Chico, California (n.d., c.1981). Other useful translations of Marx's work include *The Early Writings*, and *Selected Writings in Sociology and Social Philosophy*, both of which were edited and translated by T. B. Bottomore and for which Erich Fromm provided forewards. The original publisher was C. A. Watts and Co. (London, 1954); McGraw-Hill (New York) republished both in 1964. In 1971 McGraw-Hill issued Marx's *On Revolution* as edited and translated by Saul K. Padover. The latter is one of several volumes in McGraw-Hill's *The Karl Marx Library*.

1. "Private Property and Communism" in the Third Economic and Philosophical Manuscript, *Early Writings*, 155.
2. From Gandhi's discussion with Louis Fischer recorded in K. G. Mashruwala, *Gandhi and Marx* (Ahmedabad, India: Navajivan Publishing House, 1951), app. 3,109.
3. "Qualifying Violent Revolution," in *On Revolution*, 64.

4. *Young India*, July 17, 1924.
5. Marx's position on the necessity of violence for revolutionary change is not clear. The second international congress of communist movements, meeting in Paris in 1889, was sharply divided about the proper interpretation of Marx on this point, and Lenin's insistence on the more violent reading was a cause for schism within the ranks.
6. "Address of the Central Authority to the League," in *Collected Works*, 10:279.
7. "Zur Judenfrage," in *The Early Writings*, 20.
8. "Qualifying Violent Revolution," in *On Revolution*, 64.
9. "Communist Manifesto," in *On Revolution*, 81.
10. "Communist Manifesto," in *On Revolution*, 81.
11. "Communist Manifesto," in *On Revolution*, 81.
12. In the Marxist revolution in China, especially, many smaller landowners were reeducated rather than eliminated.
13. "The Civil War in France," in *On Revolution*, 353.
14. "Communist Manifesto," in *On Revolution*, 81.
15. *Harijan*, July, 1947.
16. *Gandhi and Marx*, 109.
17. Quoted in D. G. Tendulkar, *Mahatma: The Life of Mohandas Karamchand Gandhi* (Bombay: Jhaveri and Tendulkar, 1954), 4:15.
18. "Communist Manifesto," in *On Revolution*, 93.
19. Quoted in Tendulkar, *Mahatma*, 15.
20. "Qualifying Violent Revolution," *On Revolution*, 64.
21. "Critique of Hegel's Dialectic and General Philosophy" in the Third Economic and Philosophical Manuscript, *The Early Writings*, 211.
22. "Communist Manifesto," *On Revolution*, 107.

Issue #2: Can Anger Be True? *(Freud v. Gandhi)*

My information on Freud comes from his own writing, the most complete English collection of which is *The Standard Edition of the Complete Psychological Works of Sigmund Freud* (hereafter *Complete Psychological Works*), translated by James Strachey in collaboration with Anna Freud (London: Hogarth Press, 1964). Some of Freud's most interesting comments on war and nonviolence are contained in an exchange of letters between him and Einstein that is to be found under the heading "Why War?" in volume 22 of the collected works.

1. Erik Erikson, *Gandhi's Truth: On the Origins of Militant Nonviolence* (New York: W. W. Norton and Co., 1969), 424-5.
2. Erikson, *Gandhi's Truth*, 244-5, italics in the original.
3. Erikson, *Gandhi's Truth*, 245.
4. *Young India*, March 9, 1922.
5. *Young India*, March 9, 1922.
6. *Complete Psychological Works*, 16:294.
7. *Complete Psychological Works*, 16:294.
8. *Complete Psychological Works*, 9:35.
9. *Complete Psychological Works*, 9:35.
10. Gandhi, *Selected Works*, 6:111,155.
11. *Complete Psychological Works*, 22:209.
12. *Yeravda Mandir*, 5.
13. *Complete Psychological Works*, 22:211.
14. *Complete Psychological Works*, 22:211-12.
15. *Complete Psychological Works*, 22:214.

16. *Complete Psychological Works*, 22:212.
17. *Complete Psychological Works*, 22:213.
18. *Complete Psychological Works*, 22:203.
19. *Complete Psychological Works*, 22:215.
20. *Complete Psychological Works*, 22:204.
21. *Complete Psychological Works*, 22:211.
22. *Complete Psychological Works*, 22:205.
23. *Complete Psychological Works*, 22:213.
24. *Complete Psychological Works*, 22:213.
25. *Complete Psychological Works*, 22:215.

Issue #3: Is a Force of Love Realistic? *(Gandhi v. Niebuhr)*

In understanding Reinhold Niebuhr's thought I have been especially aided by his Gifford lectures, *The Nature and Destiny of Man* (New York: Charles Scribner's Sons, 1941); *Christian Realism and Political Problems* (New York: Charles Scribner's Sons, 1953); and *Moral Man and Immoral Society* (New York: Charles Scribner's Sons, 1932). Also useful are the essays about him collected in Charles W. Kegley and Robert W. Bretall, eds., *Reinhold Niebuhr: His Religious, Social and Political Thought* (New York: The Macmillan Co, 1961). The book concludes with a chapter in which Niebuhr responds to his critics and observers. In addition to reading Niebuhr's works, I had the good fortune of studying with him at Union Theological Seminary, New York, from 1962 to 1965.

1. Kenneth Kaunda, *The Riddle of Violence*, ed. Colin M. Morris (San Francisco: Harper and Row, 1980), 41.
2. Quoted in June Bingham, *The Courage to Change* (New York: Charles Scribner's Sons, 1961), 368.
3. Arthur Schlesinger, Jr., "Reinhold Niebuhr's Role in Political Thought," in Kegley and Bretall, *Reinhold Niebuhr*, 150.
4. The phrase is used by Ronald Stone, *Reinhold Niebuhr: Prophet to Politicians* (Washington D.C.: University Press of America, 1981).
5. *Nature and Destiny*, 1:179.
6. *Nature and Destiny*, 2:68.
7. *Nature and Destiny*, 1:179.
8. *Young India*, August 27, 1925.
9. *Moral Man*, xi-xii.
10. *Moral Man*, xii.
11. *Nature and Destiny*, 2:265.
12. *Moral Man*, 155, 194.
13. *Young India*, August 25, 1920.
14. *Moral Man*, 243.
15. *Moral Man*, 242.
16. *Moral Man*, 242.
17. *Moral Man*, 246.
18. *Moral Man*, 238.
19. *Moral Man*, 242.
20. *Young India*, November 5, 1919.
21. *Moral Man*, 244.
22. *Moral Man*, 253-4.
23. *Harijan*, October 14, 1939.
24. *Moral Man*, 255.
25. *Moral Man*, 256.

Issue #4: Was Gandhi Always a Gandhian? *(Mohandas v. the Mahatma)*

For the general outlines of Gandhi's life I have consulted the following biographies: Pyarelal, *Mahatma Gandhi*, 3 vols. (Ahmedabad, India: Navajivan Trust, 1956, 1958, and 1965), Geoffrey Ashe, *Gandhi* (New York: Stein and Day, 1968), and B. R. Nanda, *Mahatma Gandhi: A Biography* (London: Allen and Unwin, 1958). The incident about Kasturbai and the going away gifts is reported by Gandhi in his *Autobiography,* and the settlement with General Smuts is described in *Satyagraha in South Africa,* (1928; reprint, Ahmedabad, India: Navajivan Publishing House, 1961). For Gandhi's understanding of his epic fast, I have relied on volume 51 of the *Collected Works* and the account by Pyarelal in *The Epic Fast,* (Ahmedabad, India: Navajivan Publishing House, 1932). I have previously explored Gandhi's differences with the Untouchables during this incident in "The Epic Fast: A Case Study in Cross-Cultural Ethics" (paper delivered at Columbia University, April 23, 1982, for the Berkeley-Harvard Program in the Comparative Study of Social Values); and in "Mangoo Ram vs. Gandhi" in my *Religion as Social Vision: The Movement against Untouchability in 20th Century Punjab* (Berkeley and Los Angeles: University of California Press, 1982), chapter 12.

1. This is the subtitle given Gandhi's autobiography.
2. *Autobiography,* 48.
3. *Autobiography,* 112.
4. *Autobiography,* 396.
5. *Collected Works,* 51:63.
6. *Collected Works,* 59:264.
7. Ashe, *Gandhi,* 373.
8. Jawaharlal Nehru, reprinted in *Homage to Mahatma Gandhi* (New Delhi: Ministry of Information and Broadcasting, 1948), 9-10.
9. *Autobiography,* 222.
10. *Autobiography,* 221.
11. *Autobiography,* 221.
12. *Autobiography,* 222.
13. Quoted in U. S. Mohan Rao, ed., *The Message of Mahatma Gandhi* (New Delhi, India: Publication Division, Ministry of Information and Broadcasting, Government of India, 1968), 115.
14. *Autobiography,* 220.
15. *Autobiography,* 12.
16. *Autobiography,* 19.
17. Quoted in Louis Fischer, *The Essential Gandhi* (New York: Vintage Books, 1962), 179.
18. *Yeravda Mandir,* 1.
19. *Young India,* September 23, 1926.
20. *Autobiography,* 220.
21. *Young India,* September 23, 1926.
22. Ashe, *Gandhi,* 90.
23. *Young India,* June 18, 1925.
24. *Collected Works,* 33:102.
25. Quoted in *Mahatma Gandhi, Essays and Reflections on His Life and Work,* cited in Louis Fischer, *The Life of Mahatma Gandhi* (New York: Harper and Brothers, 1950), 125.
26. Ashe, *Gandhi,* 125.
27. For example, Gandhi's comments on South Africa on November 17, 1947, in his *Delhi Diary* (Ahmedabad, India: Navajivan Publishing House, 1948), 178.

28. *Young India*, September 29, 1921.
29. *Delhi Diary*, October 3, 1947.
30. *Collected Works*, 14:511.
31. *Collected Works*, 14:440.
32. *Collected Works*, 14:505.
33. *Collected Works*, 14:436.
34. *Harijan*, June 10, 1939; *Harijan*, May 12, 1946. See also Stephen Hay, "Gandhi's Views on Defensive Violence and Participation in War" (paper presented at the meetings of the American Academy of Religion, Western Region, April 8, 1983).
35. *Collected Works*, 14:444.
36. *Collected Works*, 14:485. The term *effeminate* is Gandhi's, and is typical of the gender imagery to which he often resorted in describing attitudes of weakness and strength. He frequently described an absence of courage, for example, as "a lack of manhood."
37. *Collected Works*, 51:101.
38. For Dr. B. R. Ambedkar's position, see *Dr. Ambedkar on Poona Pact* (Jullundur, India: Bheem Patrika Publications, 1973) and *What Gandhi and Congress Have Done to the Untouchables* (Bombay, 1946).
39. *Collected Works*, 51:63.
40. *Collected Works*, 51:117.
41. *Collected Works*, 51:112.
42. *Young India*, September 23, 1926.
43. *Harijan*, February 18, 1933.
44. *Collected Works*, 51:52.
45. *Harijan*, April 21, 1946.
46. *Harijan*, April 21, 1946.
47. *Harijan*, February 18, 1933.
48. *Harijan*, February 18, 1933.
49. *Collected Works*, 51:111.
50. *Harijan*, May 6, 1933.
51. *Young India*, March 11, 1927.
52. *Harijan*, May 6, 1933.
53. *Young India*, March 3, 1927.

The Issues That Remain

1. *Collected Works*, 51:17.
2. Clarence Marsh Case, *Non-Violent Coercion* (New York: Century, 1923) and Kirby Page, "Is Coercion Ever Justifiable?" *This World Tomorrow*, 15 (June 1932).
3. Kirby Page, quoted in Mulford Sibley, *The Quiet Battle* (Chicago: Quadrangle Books, 1963) 52.
4. *Young India*, May 20, 1926.

Index